Rilke's Sonnets to Orpheus

Rilke's Sonnets to Orpheus

A Translation in Sonnet Form

by

Nancy Billias

dream abbey
PUBLISHING HOUSE

Dream Abbey
4 Covewood Court
Arden, NC 28704 USA
dreamabbey.com

© 2023 Nancy Billias. All rights reserved.

Cover image: Barbara Hepworth, *Orpheus* (Maquette 2, Version II), 1956. Copper alloy and cotton string on wooden base. From the permanent collection of the Tate Gallery, St Ives, Cornwall, United Kingdom, and on permanent display in the Barbara Hepworth Museum and Sculpture Garden. Permission for use authorized by Sophie Bowness on behalf of the estate of Barbara Hepworth.

No part of this book may be reproduced or translated in any form or by any means, electronical or mechanical, including photography, recording, or by any information storage and retrieval system or technologies now known or later developed, without permission in writing from the publisher.

Printed on acid-free paper.

Library of Congress Control Number: 2023941689

ISBN 978-1-951105-08-2 (paperback)
ISBN 978-1-951105-09-9 (ebook)

*To Edward Emery,
who taught me how to listen*

Contents

Rilke's Buddha Sonnets ix

A Meditation on Translation xix

A Few Notes on the Sonnets xliii

Book I 1

Book II 55

About the Author 115

Rilke's Buddha Sonnets

Preface to the Buddha Sonnets

How auspicious! As publishers, it is our wish is to spread works that create inspiration and realization in the minds of readers, and this translation of Rilke's *Sonnets to Orpheus* by Nancy Billias is a beautiful example of the transformative power of the written word.

To date, Dream Abbey has primarily published commentaries and text translations of the Tibetan Yungdrung Bon tradition—an ancient esoteric tradition that closely resembles Tibetan Buddhism—while simultaneously remaining a publisher for poets, philosophers, and visionaries to share their revelatory perspectives.

The idealist and esoteric teachings of both East and West may help orient the reader to a clearer way of seeing the world, provide methods of self-discovery, or simply offer a moment's respite from the onslaught of problems we create for ourselves.

In his Sonnets, Rilke gives us Orpheus as a symbol of the poet's (or practitioner's) ability for self-transcendence. The creative activity of the poet brings both writer and reader to an inner experience of awareness—a goal quite in line with that of Bön and Buddhism.

From Sonnet II, 14:

> *By nature all things float, but like ballasters, we,*
> *charmed by mass, plod around encumbering*
> *all with self. What spoilers we must seem*
> *to them, in their endless childhood dream.*

Rilke here sees us as being attached and enchanted by the material objects of our world. Rather than float through existence as our true nature, we are trapped in the orbits of apparent mass and must *plod around*. Here, Rilke deftly points out that this situation isn't that we are encumbered by this mass but that we create the sense of encumberment through our disillusioned views of the world and conventional sense of self.

These compounded illusions that make up our everyday reality are, to the Tibetan sages, very much like a dream. In the Bön teachings, our true nature is endlessly spacious, infinitely energetic, and filled with the clarity of pure awareness. The variety of attachments and incorrect views that overlay this reality create the flawed, dreamlike forms and concepts that regularly display in our minds as our everyday reality.

The Inner Mirror is a commentary on the A-tri Dzogchen practices of the Bön tradition, published by Dream Abbey in 2019. In it, Latri Nyima Dakpa Rinpoche writes that according to this tradition,

> *Whatever appearances we are experiencing, they are all a kind of dream... All that we experience, sounds, feelings, taste, forms, is only momentarily there. It exists and affects us only momentarily, and then it disappears in its own way...There is no real difference, but our mind creates a difference between our daily experience and a dream, and we are circling in khorwa [(cyclical existence)] only because of a lack of understanding of the true nature, the true essence of phenomena and our own self.*

Unlike this everyday dreamlike experience, the "childhood dream" Rilke refers to in the verse above can be considered the true, unaltered form of our waking dream. For most of us, our daily lives are viewed through the stained lenses of ego, accumulated baggage, and habitual tendencies. But to those with clear vision, who see things with childlike eyes and are unencumbered by such an egoic self, "what spoilers we must seem[!]"

Eventually, when we understand the truth of our reality as a dream, we can work to transform it and discover wisdom that will benefit ourselves and others. Rilke believed in transformation and transmutation, expressing these in the form of Orpheus, who demonstrates eternal metamorphoses, and the poem itself, which is of this divine transcendence.

In II,12, Rilke writes, "He who offers himself to flow as a wellspring knows Wisdom." This view of Orpheus is quite like the highest forms of meditation, where practitioners take a mindset of radical acceptance that leaves everything, including oneself, in its own nature without modifying anything – a method that is known as "cutting through," because it cuts through the ignorant dream of conventional reality, leaving the egoic mind behind. This leads to deeper states of realization and wisdom.

Like any visionary poetry, insightful philosophy, or divine teachings, the Sonnets reveal Rilke's spirit – his will to rise above the suffering of the cyclic world and reach a state of liberation, harmony, and equilibrium.

Finally, we would be remiss to not mention Nancy Billias' own introduction, which profoundly guides the reader to a potent form of poetic meditation. Her nine steps of listening and translation offer the reader a method of entering and becoming absorbed within the text in a way that deeply resembles a spiritual experience.

Of course, the *Sonnets to Orpheus* are not inherently Buddhist. They pose their own questions and express their own unique vision. Any similarities to Bön and Buddhist concepts can most readily be found in the open minds of our readers, who, through open listening, may pass through the doorway of their own minds, and there discover their own paths to transcendence. But the Sonnets' connection with Buddhist ideas is not merely coincidental. Below, we will see a few Sonnets Rilke wrote specifically about the Buddha and Buddha nature.

- Nick Tichawa, Dream Abbey

An extract from a letter by Rilke to his wife regarding the Buddha Sonnets:

Soon after dinner I retire, at half-past eight [I] am finally back in my cottage. Then before me is the vast blossoming starry night, and below, in front of the window, the gravel path climbs a small hill, upon which, in tremendous silence, a Buddha-portrait rests, in quiet reticence imparting the unsayable containment of his gestures under all the skies of day and night. C'est le centre du monde, I said to Rodin. And then he looks at me so endearingly, in utter friendship. That is very fine and a great deal.

- Rilke to Clara Rilke-Westhoff, Meudon, 20.09.1905. Rainer Maria Rilke, Auguste Rodin, *Der Briefwechsel und andere Dokumente zu Rilkes Begegnung mit Rodin*, ed. Rätus Luck (Frankfurt am Main: Insel Verlag, 2001), pp. 111-112.

Additional background on the Buddha Sonnets:

Rilke wrote three poems on the Buddha that appear at different places within the two parts of his New Poems (Neue Gedichte), which were published in 1907 and 1908 respectively and include some of his most cherished poems – among them 'The Panther' and 'Archaic Torso of Apollo'. The first two poems in these translations are contained in the first part (Neue Gedichte). The third poem on the Buddha assumes a special importance in that it concludes the second part (Der Neuen Gedichte anderer Teil) and thus the collection.

These poems instantiate a significant cross-cultural and intermedial dialogue between West and East, Europe and Asia, sculpture and poetry, the founder of Buddhism and a Modernist poet. Rilke's interest in the Buddha was stirred by an Indonesian statue in Auguste Rodin's garden in Meudon, which the French sculptor had procured (along with other Buddha statues) from the 1900 World Expo in Paris. From September 1905 until the spring of 1906, Rilke lived in a cottage in Rodin's garden and worked as his private secretary.

Translation continues the process of intercultural dialogue. It engages in a conversation with the original text and calls for interpretation and sacrifices. Unlike a prosaic or scientific text, every aspect of a poem contributes to its meaning: diction, images, rhythm, form, tone etc. Due to the unique complexity of a given poem, its translation cannot render a perfect equivalent in the target language.

- Luke Fischer, Cordite Poetry Review, 12 October, 2012.

Rilke's Buddha Sonnets

I

It's as if he were listening. Silence: so deep, so far.
Though we can no longer hear it, we too listen.
Now he is starlight, and the unseen stars
range themselves round him: he is one with them,

encompassing all that is. Oh, do we, truly,
wait to be seen? Could this be what he needs?
Even if we flung ourselves at his feet,
he would remain deep in himself, like a dumb beast.

For that which pulls us towards him has already been
coursing in him for millions of years. In him:
who has forgotten what we undergo,
though what has banished us, he knows.

II

Even from far off, one can sense the force
of this golden pilgrim – so reserved and strange -
it's as if rueful rich men, from remorse,
heaped all their secret treasures in one place.

But – one would go nearly mad if he should try
to approach the majesty of that fearsome brow.
For these are no mere glass shards that round us lie,
Nor just some girlish earrings we see now.

If only we were able now to tell
which things were smelted down for there
to be this statue, set within the bell
of this flower: more mute, more tinged to glow
with peace than gold, stirring the very air
through which it moves, as if it were its own.

III

Hail, core of all cores, heart at the heart
of all, nut that enfolds all sweetness
in itself, - to the end of the stars
the flesh of your fruit reaches.

Now, you can feel how you are utterly free,
as the sap surges, presses through
the shell which stretches to infinity,
even as its force streams out to you.

Far, far overhead, your suns will spin
backwards in the sky, in full, radiant glow.
And so it is: for in you, long since,
that which alone will survive them all arose.

A Meditation on Translation

Nancy Billias

Like all language, this book is an attempt at communication. Communication is always in the process of translation, even between those who share a common set of meaning-making symbols (words and phrases), because language must always traverse the narrow and perilous bridge between minds, between seemingly individual selves.

When we say something, or translate something, it is never a matter, really, of accomplishing meaning, but rather of moving towards meaning. As I understand it, this movement begins with taking a stance of openness, of opening ourselves to the possibility of meaning, of coming to a place where meaning might be discovered. Through language, we seek to define the space between ourselves and the others who make up our world, in order to find meaning. In our fear of finding nothing in that space, too often we close ourselves off to openness: we look to language not to discover, but to invent meaning. We think of ourselves as the makers of meaning rather than its observers and participants.

In so doing, I think we often miss a significant opportunity. Instead of seeking an open space, we use words – in whatever language or form – to create enclosed, defined areas, which block us from entering more deeply into an understanding of the interconnected nature of all being. It is my belief that listening more closely to language in translation can show us a path towards meaning.

In addition, I believe that poetic language can be particularly helpful in the task of turning ourselves towards meaning. The *vers* within 'verse' implies both turn and proximity.[i] Poetic language, in its fluidity and instability, helps us to turn our focus, and so may bring us closer to immersion in the fullness of interconnected being.

Within language as a whole, poetic language has a unique trajectory. The path of its flight unfolds as the poem participates in, listens to the event which it describes. Thus, poetic language is already a form of translation. To paraphrase the first of Rilke's Orphic Sonnets, poetic language rises to the ear, comes forward to be heard. Like the Buddhist concept of enlightenment, it is a revelation of what is already present, of what lies waiting in the experience of the everyday to be disclosed and brought into presence. Like enlightenment, the meaning of a poem is not a destination to be arrived at. It is always already there.

In the Orphic Sonnets, Rilke assigns to poetry and to poets the task of listening, of occupying a space of open receptivity, a task which is not so much an activity but a state of being – again, like the act of meditation.

A MEDITATION ON TRANSLATION

Let's take Rilke's suggestion one step further. Suppose we think about translation as a very specific type of listening, even more specific than poetry. It might be said that any translation is a form of poetic language, simultaneously a type of poetic listening and poetic speaking. Understood in this way, translation might be thought of as a form of meditation: it is not about achieving a goal or reaching an end-point. Rather, in relation to both language and meaning, translation is a liminal state, a condition of between-ness: between what has been said and what is about to be heard, in the apparent gaps between individual points of consciousness.

If we think of language as an act of listening, and translation as a very specific form of listening, what then is the character of a translated word? Understood as an exercise in listening to language, rather than as a product, the process of translation teaches us that the condition under which anything can be said to exist is a condition of sheer indeterminacy. Seen in this way, translation stands outside of, otherwise than, linear time. It makes no sense to speak of translation in terms of linear time; there is no end to the process of translation. There is no end, just as there was no beginning. There is no perfect original, of which the translator makes a more or less faithful copy. Rather, there is a performance in one language, a performance in another language, and the interpretation and interior understanding of each reader. To continue to expect a perfect translation of a poem is absurd. The analogy of music is never far away from poetry; translation is as ephemeral as the performance of a piece of music, equally only a glimpse, a snapshot of the idea of the music, equally separate from time.

The parallel to meditation seems obvious here. The activity of listening – whether listening to language in the act of translation, or by listening to being in the act of meditation – is not a dance of many veils, wherein meaning (or truth) will eventually be revealed in its full and naked splendour. Rather, in both cases, flashes of splendour, of fullness, occur. In translation, one does not begin with an original text. (It might even be impossible to say that an original exists, since it exists only to be heard, only as a point of departure for a colloquy with other subjects. Thus, an original exists only in the same way that a translation exists: as a performative moment.) Because of the non-linear nature of the processes of translation and meditation, one cannot even say that one begins. The revelation (if any) of meaning (if any) takes place outside of, separate from linear time. It occurs, comes briefly into manifestation, and then it is gone again. The *movement* of being, as it is revealed either through meditation or translation, cannot be contained within the confines of linear time.

Both translation and meditation show us at least two ways in which the fullness of being reveals and manifests itself. First is an apophatic revelation (from *apophatikos*, negative). That is, what is revealed is only what something is not. Revealing the space around an object is a way of clearly defining the parameters and shape of the object. The term comes from early Christian theology, which sought to provide a definition for an invisible and essentially unknowable God by eliminating attributes which were logically incompatible with a definition of a uniquely supreme being.

In this respect, language in translation shares an essential characteristic with poetic language and with the transcendental aim of meditation. The poetic character of translation manifests itself around a promise of what cannot be contained in what is immediately present. The poetic character of translation is encapsulated in the moment of the *caesura,* the momentary pause before a word is spoken and heard. In the silent space of the *caesura,* the parameters of what is said and heard are clearly defined. Understood as the science of the *caesura,* translation might be seen as an essential component of the process of communication. The 'loss' that occurs in translation may serve to define the negative silhouette by which the essence of a text is revealed in greater clarity. By revealing what is not being said, the space around meaning which falls away in translation may define the parameters and shape of the poem anew.

Another way in which both translation and meditation can reveal the fullness of being is kairologically. This term is also borrowed from early Christian (Patristic) theology. *Kairos* (meaning 'right' or 'proper') is the ripening of manifestation within its own good time; the most apt and fortuitous moment for an event, for the performance of an action, or for the coming into being of a new state. It is the moment of the fulfilment of hope. In translation, as in meditation, the fullness of being manifests itself kairologically, as and when it will, in response to the openness of the listener.

Seen in this way, both meditation and translation can be understood as acts of promise and hope. As such, I would argue, translation becomes language at its most apophatic and kairological, while meditation is human activity at its most apophatic and kairological. Through these actions, one may discover what lies hidden, in language, or in human potentiality. Like meditation, translation neither gives birth to meaning nor mirrors a pre-existing meaning. There is no point of origin or point of departure for a meditation (for a translation), but only what emerges from the fullness of being in the moment, for the moment. The movement of translation, of meditation, carries what lies hidden forward and across dichotomies, polarities, and gaps, to new presence.

Both activities reveal the relative meaninglessness of the rational concepts of linear time and teleology, because the fullness of being manifests itself so clearly, in its own way, in its own time, and often by means of silence – not according to reason, not in any metaphysical line, but as response to openness. What translation – or meditation – offers is a non-linear proof (or trace) of the fullness of being: as *remainder* - what is always *left over* in the course of an intersubjective exchange or manifestation – and as *essence* – what is *always* left over. Since the fullness of being is itself non-linear, one cannot expect it to manifest in linear, rational fashion. A hidden, indeterminable trace of its essence is left behind; its essence as hope remains always to be discovered anew.

The indeterminable condition, whether or language or of being, does not imply blurriness, but rather a state of discovering that which is concealed: hidden presence, rather than utter absence. Similarly, the existence of translation outside of or separate from time does not imply suspension. The movement of fullness which is elucidated, brought to light, whether by translation or by meditation is absolutely not a state of suspended animation. It is not about the suspension of a state of being; rather, about its opposite: perpetual fluidity. As promise, as hope, translation re-presents the fluid motion of language. Meditation as promise, as hope, represents the fluid motion of human potentiality. These are movements that can never find stasis, because being is always recreating itself in newness, manifesting itself ever and again in response to openness.

As listening, translation or meditation may seem to be bridges, but they are not bridges between two fixed points. Rather, the bridge itself *is* a destination, a place of meaning. Yet it is not a place either; it cannot be located in place any more than in time. It is a clearing, a space that is pure openness, an opening into the Open.

Thus, both activities are always on the verge of withdrawal: for translation, withdrawal from an original, from the author, from the translator; for meditation, withdrawal from the present, from the meditator. For either activity, the point is always slipping away. Thus, we do not find our way to meaning – whether the meaning of a particular text or the meaning of a particular point in life – with a once-for-all translation. Rather, all of a sudden, a glimpse of meaning looms. But equally, it is not a moment of teleological fulfilment, because we can never come to the end of meaning. There is always more. There is always a remainder of meaning that is, truly, essentially untranslatable and mysterious.

Translator of Tibetan Buddhism Ken McLeod writes that his goal is always to bring the reader to a moment of awakening:

> *Ideally, when I translate a text, the translation elicits an experience in the reader that is at least an echo of what I experience when I read the original...At each step I have*

chosen clear meaning and experiential impact over literal accuracy.[ii]

I see many parallels between the activities of translation – specifically poetry translation - and meditation, and I find Rilke's Orphic sonnets to be a particularly apt expression of some of these parallels. For example, these poems speak simultaneously of presence and transcendence. Rilke calls on the mundane – fish and dogs, earthenware plates, flowers, pulsing engines – to draw us beyond them as individual objects and beyond our understanding of ourselves as discrete egos. In an essay on Rilke's poetry, Karlheinz Fingerhut (a scholar of German literature) spoke of Rilke's embodiment of the poetic vocation. I hear in Fingerhut's description deep echoes of the experience of meditation, which has both unique and universal aspects.

> *By a gradual loosening or transcendence of its own forms, the poem strives to escape from the linear, denotative, logically determined bonds of linguistic syntax into what the poet takes to be the simultaneities, immediacies, and free play of musical form...the poet hopes to find the paradox resolved of an act of creation singular to the creator, bearing the shape of his own spirit, yet infinitely renewed in each listener.*[iii]

Fingerhut defines the vocation of the poet as a seer, a visionary who looks beyond the here-and-now into what lies beyond and between our singular experiences of the world. Scholars from other disciplines have also pointed to Rilke's remarkable ability to translate the experience of transcendence in this way. For example, the Italian philosopher and psychoanalyst Gemma Corradi Fiumara writes:

> *The sensibility of the poet descends deep into the realm of the unsayable, where there is such an unmediated relationship between things that a language of mutual comprehension, such as humans have, is unnecessary. The muteness of the fish [in Sonnet II, 20] is a symbol for relationships which do not require words...*[iv]

Here again, as with the *caesura*, as in meditation, we meet silence. Not now as a pause between words, but as an entirely different way of being. Like meditation, Rilke's poetry allows us to look across the seemingly unbridgeable gap between individual minds into the abyss of being itself.

In a meditation on translation, the German philosopher Martin Heidegger suggests that all poetry contains this quality.

> *The poetry of a poet or the treatise of a thinker stands within its own proper unique word. It compels us to perceive this word again and again as if we were hearing it for the first time. These newborn words transpose us in every case to a new shore.*[v]

In poetry, in translation, in meditation, the possibilities inherent in being are always present, waiting for us on the other shore. All we have to do is listen. But the act of listening demands that we let go of what we think we know in order to hear something new. It demands that we step out into the abyss, into what Heidegger called *Lichtung* (the illuminative clearing within which thought, meaning or presence can occur) and what Rilke called 'the Open'. This kind of listening can, in the act of translation, bring language into new presence, and in meditation, can bring *us* into presence, into fulfillment, perhaps even into enlightenment.

Stages of Listening, Stages of Translation

For me, poetry translation is not only a way of listening for meaning, but also a form of hermeneutics: a way of seeking and interpreting meaning. Corradi Fiumara believes that listening is the starting point of hermeneutics.

Corradi Fiumara sees an explicit and express link between the processes of listening for and interpreting meaning.[vi] Further, she shows how the notion of hermeneutic listening is Rilke's goal:

> *The message from the other will not attain its expressive potential except in the context of a relationship through which the listening interlocutor actually becomes a participant in the nascent thought of the person who is talking. But a listener can only "enter" in a way which is at once paradoxical and committing: by "taking leave," by standing aside and making room. The type of listening which can be transmuted into a process of birth and growth may perhaps find expression in the language of Rilke: "If*

A MEDITATION ON TRANSLATION

> *you want to make a tree grow, surround it with the interior space which you have in yourself...Only in your own renunciation can it take form and become truly a tree.*[vii]

For Corradi Fiumara, this type of attention brings the long-ignored 'other side' of language (listening) into sharp relief, and so can bring us a long way towards re-balancing discourse, which has become a moribund and perverted activity. She argues that listening can put us back on the path towards genuine communication. She also draws on the theologian Paul Ricoeur's counsel that we can establish a right relationship of the will towards the other through listening:

> *We should start out from a point of view in which the autonomy of our will is rooted in a dependency...which is not contaminated by accusation, prohibition or sanction. Listening itself creates such a pre-ethical situation; it is a way of being which is not yet a way of doing, and because of this it escapes from the alternative of submission or revolt.*[viii]

Precisely this attitude of interdependence is the stance from which to begin a translation – or a meditation. I have isolated nine stages involved in the way in which I go about listening to and translating a poem. I offer these as a prelude to the sonnets. Each step is also a stage of listening. These same steps are, I believe, common to meditation or to any inquiry into meaning. In outlining these stages here, I will make reference to them only in terms of my process of translation, leaving the parallels for you to explore.

1. Approaching with an attitude of 'being towards'
2. Entering the poem (leaving ego behind)
3. Breathing the rhythm of the poem
4. Being filled with the essence of the poem
5. Hearing the words of the original
6. Searching for the name
7. Apprehending the whole: 'Being with' the poem
8. Being pushed away
9. Returning to a new place

1. Approaching with an attitude of 'being towards'

To begin with, I have a neutral standpoint: I simply approach the text in an attitude of being open towards it. I wait to see what might be hidden within it. As I move through the process, I must continue to keep myself receptive, without seeking to make any premature cognitive links. If I wait for the text to come to me, Corradi Fiumara promises, something new will occur, an act of creation brought about by the act of listening.

> *The symbolic fruition of the message...allows for the emergence of something authentically and unthinkably interesting [inter-esse, among and in the midst of things, at the centre of a thing] that is not to be found already waiting in the object – text or message: it is disclosed because radical and dedicated listening engenders the resonances, recombinations and developments that only derive from a condition of germinal acceptance.[ix]*

The attitude of open receptivity draws forth newness, makes the clearing. This begins neither as a matter of knowledge or perception, but simply as a matter of being towards. The translator approaches the poem with the intention to bring it to new life in a new language, to turn it in a new version, a new moment of presence. But there are risks involved in the attitude of openness required by listening. Looking into any text means letting it confront me, and perhaps confound me.

> *Wishing to pursue the "objectively correct" teaching of Heraclitus mean refusing to run the salutary risk of being confounded by the truth of a thinking.*[x]

To translate, I must be willing to run that risk; to be open to the challenges to my usual definition of the world which the poem may present.

2. Entering the Poem

The Italian philosopher Michele Sciacca wrote: "*To communicate is to enter the other, while watching ourselves carefully, to enter without usurping...*"[xi] This description of communication holds true for my efforts at translation; the difference is that my 'other' is not a person, but a text, a poem.

Entering the text, entering into relationship with the text places me in a position of responsibility towards it: the text becomes (to borrow a term from the French philosopher Emmanuel Levinas) a face to whom I must respond; by my listening presence with(in) the text, I make a commitment to bring the text back into presence. The whole process bespeaks an ethical reciprocity. Listening leads to being with. 'Being-with others develops in listening to one another.'[xii] The imaginal space in which new meaning can come forward is the space vacated, left free by the ego.

3. Breathing the Rhythm

The next necessary step is to breathe the rhythm of the poem. This stage moves me from the interactive realm of the ethical into a place that is at once closer to the centre of the poem and to my own centre. Now the poem is not a face, but a breath which sustains me, a current on which I am carried deeper into the poem's essence. In this breath I begin to understand the concept of *Weltinnenraum*, the notion of infinite interior space which was so important to Rilke as he moved towards writing the *Sonnets* (and which is already present in the early Buddha sonnets, which appear in this book). I begin to sense the *Weltinnenraum* of the poem as both a separate entity and a shareable space, a space in which I too can participate. (The first sonnet of Book II is particularly relevant to this point, as is I, 3.)

I cannot name the breath which blows in and through the poem: is it 'a divine inspiration' or merely the sighing of wind through emptiness? In either case, as I continue to breathe the poem's rhythm, the poignancy of the link almost overwhelms me. How fragile and tenuous the hold of the poem on presence. And mine.

Breathing in the rhythm of the poem, I feel the invitation extended by the poem to the translator to enter its world. It is an invitation at once public and intimate, an invitation without words and yet made up of the words of the poem. This is more than an invitation to read; it is an invitation to become a part of the poetic itself, to enter the being of the poem.

4. Being Filled

In the next phase, the self of the translator drops away as the poem completely fills the interior space. It is as though I have entered a room, and closing the door behind me, discovered myself underwater, completely submerged in the poem. Nothing exists but the world named by the poem. In the process of being named, the poem stakes its claim on the translator, engulfs the translator in the disclosure of the poem's being present. Being filled with the poem's essence, with the poem as essence, means self-forgetfulness. Immersing self in the world of the poem, I lose the sense of where the poem's edges end and mine begin. The sensation is very close to that of meditation. It is not a matter of will. It is a matter of completely dropping out of oneself into the other; in this case, into the poem. One does not accomplish this by an act of will; rather, one is compelled, and one surrenders.[xiii] What occurs is a quiet and instantly impenetrable immediacy, a unity of identity that is both fluid and potentially drowning, under the spell of which the translator's identity no longer seems to signify.[xiv] It is swift, sudden, and total. One is swept in pre-reflectively. Opening myself to being swept away, I am instantly in the rhythm and sway of the poem, swimming in the struggle to make it right, as resonant in translation as it is in its first language.

The intense act of listening in which the translator is engaged has a profound effect on both translator and translated. In her account of learning to live in a second language, Eva Hoffman describes a similar experience in translating poetry. She writes:

> ...*that's what it's like to play the piano, in those moments when I can no longer tell whether I'm playing the music or the music is playing me...I have only the vaguest idea, and by the time I look up these words in a dictionary and accomplish the translation from the sounds to their definition, it's hard to reinsert them into the flow of the lines, the seamless sequence of musical meaning. I concentrate intensely, too intensely, and the lines come out straight and square, though I intuit a meaning that's only an inflection away. And so I struggle harder to enter the stanza, like a frustrated lover whose hunger is fed by the inaccessible proximity of her object.*[xv]

Her experience, she says, is that of language speaking 'from the cells', the words at first seeming to refer only to themselves, then gradually becoming more and more clear, even as her own identity dissolves into the translation.

5. Hearing the Words

At length I am ready to hear the words of the original poem. Through those words, a world must first be named, the world which the poet constructed in the poem. As the translator struggles under the yoke with the poem, to draw the world of the poem into the translator's own world, names emerge. In each case, it is a very particular name, a name that can apply only here-and-nowhere-else, partaking of and at the same time constituting the here-and-now of the original and the translation. Even a very common word (for example, the word 'and') or a space (a rhythmic beat) can emerge as a name for a particular moment with the poem, and immediately becomes a part of the movement that is bringing the poem to the new shore. This name does not substitute for the previous, 'original' word; it does not stand for or stand in for it. It re-presents it, in terms of bringing the word of the poem into presence in the here-and-now of the translator, and if it is the 'right' name, its own proper name, it will bring the poem into presence in the here-and-now of the reader.

6. Searching for the Name

At some point the search for the name engages the conscious mind of the translator: the bridging knowledge of both languages; the desire to bring the word into presence in a new form. After all this making-ready I can finally use all my linguistic skills and knowledge. This activity begins as anything but transparency: it begins as apprehension of a brightly-colored and carefully-crafted tapestry from which the translator must isolate each thread without disturbing the whole. Any pulling on the weave is immediately apparent; its rough edges seem to catch on my skin.

To change metaphors, on the one side is the smooth brilliance of the poem itself: an organized composition of color, shade, and light, a still life. This side of the text is like the mirror-surface reflecting the world in which the poem was originally produced. On the other side of the poem, the translator stacks neat and equally color-rich reserves of information and imagery, knowledge of poetic syntax, awareness of the poet's affinities, influences, style, mannerisms. But from where does the translation appear, and how does all this color, all this accumulated 'stuff' become transparent? The answer emerges in the next phase, when the translator moves from isolating the threads within the poem back to an apprehension of the poem as a whole.

7. Apprehending the Whole: Being with the Poem

The shift which began to occur through listening prepared a blankness within the translator. Now this negative space in the translator becomes (or rather, is) the diaphanous canvas onto which the translation emerges. As the translation comes into presence, each particular name (word or beat) transfers itself from the original to the translation, through the unresisting agency of the translator. That is, in fact, all the translator has to do: not resist the movement that brings the original poem into the here-and-now of the translation, in the fullness of time, into the fullness of presence. To be present with the poem, in its presence.

Such inactivity, of course, is extremely difficult, as anyone who has attempted any form of meditation will recognize. 'All' that is required is that the ego drop away into the clear stream of being that is constantly flowing through one. In the process of translation, the translator listens not only (one might almost say, 'not ever') to the poem as a whole, but rather to each particular word and beat within the poem. Each one must first be evaluated as a name, weighted, assayed for individual fidelity and value, and then listened to again in relation to the phrase or line. This procedure happens with each and every word and beat. First one, then two or a small group; gradually the pieces that are listened to together become larger and larger. Only at the very end of the procedure does one step back and hear the whole, as one would hear a piece of music rather than notes or chords, because it is only then that it exists as something 'to-be-heard'.

8. Being Pushed Away

The translator listens to the translated poem over and over again until no rough edges remain, and the poem begins to push the translator away.[xvi] At this point the translation is no longer something either poet or translator is saying, not something to-be-said or to-be-heard, but simply something that *is* heard. Now the poem exists independently in the here-and-now of the hearer.

When I go back to a translation, there comes a moment when I feel as though I am viewing it from a remove, as through a screen. I am no longer a part of it. It is detached and gone from me. I can still appreciate the pull of its beauty, but the invitation is no longer there to enter it in the same way. In fact, it resists me. From this vantage point I have no idea how the translation was accomplished; I only know that I once stood inside the poem, and now I am outside of it. This does not mean that I have produced 'the' perfect translation. What it means is that I have been dismissed; there appears to be nothing more I can do at that moment. Over time, more nuances and errors may appear, and the poem may let me back in for further work. But an uncanny feeling that I am at the poem's disposal is very strong.

9. Returning to a New Place

An overquoted stanza from T. S. Eliot is too apt to disregard here; it so completely expresses the feeling of having completed a translation:

> *We shall not cease from exploration*
> *And the end of all our exploring*
> *Will be to arrive where we started*
> *And know the place for the first time.*[xvii]

Having left the poem, I return to myself, and find that through the agency of the poem I have discovered a new and expanded definition of myself. In the course of the translation, both the poem and the translator have become translucent. The poem, in that through the light that the poem sheds on or towards meaning, some barriers of language have been overcome. The translator becomes translucent too, striving not to block the light of meaning from shining through the poem, struggling to 'be' in relation to the poem *only* as the canvas on which its new shape takes form. Not as creator, not even as co-creator, but merely as conduit, receiver. In this way, the translator comes to be as much the raw material, the 'stuff' of which the translation is composed, as is the original text itself.[xviii] In the moment of translation, the translator is completely self-transcendent. There is no room for self; the entire self of the translator is given over to the task of listening. Yet in the process the translator is not annihilated. Rather (apophatically), the negative spaces left by the process of translation contribute to the formation of a new and expanded self-understanding.

It is in this stage that I more clearly apprehend how the event of translation points the way towards human transcendence. Translating language is a vehicle (one might almost say a metaphor) for the possibility of transcendence. As language translates the experiences of beings in the world, the act of translation reveals fundamental truths of the human experience, which include both our finitude and our capacity for transcendence.

At the same time, the act of translation reveals something significant about being. The fullness of being cannot be contained within a constructed set of finite factors and variables; both its form and its content are infinitely vast and constantly shifting, free of such constraints as human reason, time, and death. We, as finite beings, finding ourselves in the midst of this free and seemingly random movement, struggle to find or establish meaning in our particular circumstances. The search for meaning inserts us into the greater context of being, and so in some way serves to guarantee meaning. The act of translation reveals some of this struggle and this state of affairs, by providing moments when the fullness of being manifests and reveals itself. That has been the challenge and the joy of this project.

Notes

[i] See Marc Froment-Meurice, *That is to Say: Heidegger's Poetics* (Palo Alto, CA: Stanford University Press), 7.

[ii] Ken McLeod, "Inside the Translator's Workbook: An Exploration of Three Lines That Hit the Nail on the Head", *Tricycle Review,* Fall 2020, Vol 30: 1.

[iii] Karlheinz Fingerhut, *Das Kreaturliche im Werke R. M. Rilkes: Untersuchungen zur Figur des Tieres* (Bonn: Bouvier, 1970), 146.

[iv] Gemma Corradi Fiumara, *The Other Side of Language: A Philosophy of Listening.* (London: Routledge, 1995), 79.

[v] Martin Heidegger, *Parmenides* (Bloomington: Indiana University Press, 1998), 12.

[vi] "One of the most important aspects of listening is in fact discernible when cognitive frontiers are opened up without any 'frontal' attack, but only in relation to our availability to listen rigorously; as if our determination to go forward tentatively without knowing exactly our direction, but sustained by the readiness to listen…were exactly what opens the way for the birth of thought. In the readiness to understand there is precisely an effort to follow up the inner consequentiality of someone's expressions: the disposition which gives life to a 'listening event'. The thing experienced itself becomes capable of utterance insofar as the interlocutor adheres to a rationality which is capable not only of saying but above all of listening, and insofar as the interlocutor opens himself to the strength of thought springing to life in the other, free from the cognitive claims provided by his own interpretative parameters." Corradi Fiumara, *op.cit.*, 143ff.

[vii] *Ibid.*, 144ff.

[viii] Paul Ricoeur, quoted in Corradi Fiumara, *The Other Side of Language*, 149.

ABOUT THE TRANSLATOR

[ix] Corradi Fiumara, *op.cit.*, 122.

[x] Heidegger, *What is Called Thinking?* (New York: Harper Perennial Modern Thought, 1963), 238-239.

[xi] Michele Sciacca, *El silencio y la palabra: como se vence en Waterloo.* (Barcelona: Editorial Luis Miracle, 1961), 60.

[xii] Heidegger, *Being and Time* (Oxford: Wiley-Blackwell, 1967), 206.

[xiii] See Sonnet I, 5.

[xiv] In Lewis Carroll's *Through the Looking Glass*, Alice has a similar experience. When she enters the wood where things have no names, she forgets her own. As long as she remains there, she is able to remain at one with a fawn, communing peaceably. As soon as they reach the edge of the wood, the fawn remembers both her name and its own, and bounds away in fear. The name of the translator must be forgotten. (Boston: International Pocket Library, 1941), 111- 112

[xv] Eva Hoffman, *Lost in Translation: A Life in a New Language* (New York: Random House, 2011), 180.

[xvi] This movement of pushing away reminds me of the Fort-Da game noted by Freud and Klein, wherein the toddler pushes away from the mother in order to celebrate both its autonomy and its ability to reconnect with the mother at will.

[xvii] T.S. Eliot, *Little Gidding* (London: Faber & Faber, 1942), lines 245ff.

[xviii] The same process may be said to occur in any artistic endeavor.

A Few Notes on the Sonnets

I leave to others a deeper exploration of the many intricate allusions of Rilke's imagery. I particularly recommend in this regard the notes which accompany C. F. MacIntyre's 1960 translation (University of California Press), which was the last sonnet-form translation to appear in print until now. His notes are extremely detailed and well-researched. Here I merely point out a few especially obscure references, distinguish a few of the main themes and identify the addressee of each sonnet, where this might be helpful.

The most striking characteristic of the Orphic Sonnets were also their most challenging aspect for translation: Rilke rarely if ever conformed to any traditional rhyme scheme of sonnet form. In fact, he used every possible variation. With regard to meter, most of the time Rilke hews closely to iambic pentameter, although he sometimes (I, 9, 17, 18, 19) attenuates the meter, so that the iambic pentameter usually found in one line is spread over two lines. He also occasionally (e.g., II, 17), gives a slight polyrhythmic twist that musicians will recognize as 'two against three', in which the stress always lands on the same beat of the line, although the lines have different numbers of beats. Rilke was also not averse to creating new words – quite a challenge for a translator. My over-riding goal was to preserve the musicality of the poems.

Throughout the Sonnets, the subject is always shifting, for Rilke is telling several stories at once. In addition to the myth of Orpheus (outlined briefly below), the Sonnets are dedicated to and refer in several places to the short life of Vera Ouckama Knoop, the daughter of some friends of Rilke's, who died of leukaemia at age 19. (Another sonnet, II, 8, is dedicated to a cousin of Rilke's, Egon von Rilke, who was the model for Malte Laurids Brigge)

Many of the sonnets address Orpheus directly. In addition, another theme which they consider is the vocation of the poet – which Heidegger also addressed in his 1946 essay '*Wozu Dichter?*' Quoting from the iconic German poet Hölderlin, Heidegger asks: 'What are poets for, in desperate times?' Heidegger's answer and Rilke's answer are strikingly similar, though of course expressed quite differently. For Heidegger, the poet is an embodiment of *Dasein*, the bridge of consciousness between the beings of the world (*das Seiende*) and being itself (*das Sein*). Poetic language holds open the tension of being, creating and maintaining a space in which 'what is' can manifest itself ever more fully. For Rilke, the task of the poet (in the figure of Orpheus) is to praise: to be so fully immersed in the beings of the world that being itself emerges for all to encounter.

The myth of Orpheus has three distinct moments which recur here and there throughout the Sonnets:

- The power of Orpheus' poetry is revealed in its magical effects on plants, animals, and the king of the underworld. No one and nothing is immune from its spell.
- Eurydice is allowed to follow Orpheus out of Hades on condition that he have enough faith not to turn around. As the couple emerges from the underworld, Orpheus turns to look at Eurydice, and she instantly vanishes back into Hades. (Rilke gives a greatly expanded version of this aspect of the legend in his poem 'Orpheus – Eurydice – Hermes', which appeared in 1904.)
- After this disaster, Orpheus retires heartbroken to an isolated spot. He is discovered there by the Bacchae, who tear his body to pieces. They throw his body into the water, but the timeless nature of poetry means that his singing is not silenced by his death.

Book I

I, 1

Da stieg ein Baum. O reine Übersteigung!
O Orpheus singt! O hoher Baum im Ohr!
Und alles schwieg. Doch selbst in der Verschweigung
ging neuer Anfang, Wink und Wandlung vor.

Tiere aus Stille drangen aus den klaren
gelösten Wald von Lager und Genist;
und da ergab sich, daß sie nicht aus List
und nicht aus Angst in sich so leise waren

sondern aus Hören. Brüllen, Schrei, Geröhr,
schien klein in ihren Herzen. Und wo eben
kaum eine Hütte war, dies zu empfangen,

ein Unterschlupf aus dunkelstem Verlangen,
mit einem Zugang, dessen Pfosten beben –
da schufst du ihnen Tempel im Gehör.

BOOK I

I, 1[1]

A tree arising. There. (What pure excess!
The song of Orpheus!) Soaring in the ear,
then: silence. And, within that emptiness,
beckonings to change, to birth, appeared.

The animals of silence stole forth then
perfectly still, not hunted, not in prey,
But in a rapt, attentive hearkening they
emerged from quiet forest, nest and den

to listen. Noises hot with threat or fear
now died within their hearts, and even where
there'd stood a shelter of dark animal dreams,

a refuge built of longing, with tottering beams,
dark mouth of some forgotten mine – just there,
you built your temple, deep within the ear.

---

[1] This first sonnet refers to the legendary music of Orpheus, so compelling that it could charm all living creatures. The theme recurs in the penultimate sonnet of Book II, where even trees fall under the spell of the divine song, and begin to dance to its melody. The first sonnet of Book I and the final sonnet of Book II can be understood as parentheses around the whole work. In the first poem, the reader's attention is drawn to a specific point – 'there' – where the tree of Orpheus arises. The final poem resolves this long cadence: the final line brings the reader's focus right to where we are: here.

I, 2

Und fast ein Mädchen wars, und ging hervor
aus diesem einigen Glück von Sang und Leier
und glänzte klar durch ihre Frühlingsschleier
und machte sich ein Bett in meinem Ohr

Und schlief in mir. Und alles war ihr Schlaf.
Die Bäume, die ich je bewundert, diese
fühlbare Ferne, die gefühlte Wiese
und jedes Staunen, das mich selbst betraf.

Sie schlaf die Welt. Singender Gott, wie hast
du sie vollendet, daß sie nicht begehrte,
erst wach zu sein? Sieh, sie erstand und schlief.

Wo ist ihr Tod? O wirst du dies Motiv
erfinden noch, eh sich dein Lied verzehrte? –
Wo sinkt sie hin aus mir?... Ein Mädchen fast...

I, 2[2]

A child, yet child no longer, she appeared,
born of the kiss of melody on lyre.
Like bright sun through spring mist she gleamed, afire,
and made herself a bed inside my ear

and slept within me. So enfolding all
in sleep: beloved trees, the fields
and barely felt horizons, all that in me yields
to wonder, each enrapturing thrall.

She wrapped the world in sleep. O god of song,
how was it you composed her never to stir,
to wake? See – she arose in sleep.

Her death? Can you discover that motif
before your song consumes itself, and her?
She sinks, falls from me…where?…A child no longer…

---

[2] Whilst the first sonnet was addressed directly to Orpheus, this sonnet brings Vera to the fore.

I, 3

Ein Gott vermags. Wie aber, sag mir, soll
ein Mann ihm folgen durch die schmale Leier?
sein Sinn ist Zwiespalt. An der Kreuzung zweier
Herzwege steht kein Tempel für Apoll.

Gesang, wie du ihn lehrst, ist nicht Begehr,
nicht Werbung um ein endlich noch Erreichtes;
Gesang ist Dasein. Für den Gott ein Leichtes.
Wann aber sind wir? Und wann wendet er

an unser Sein die Erde und die Sterne?
Dies ists nicht, Jüngling, dass du liebst, wenn auch
die Stimme dann den Mund dir aufstößt, – lerne

vergessen, daß du aufsangst. Das verrinnt.
In Wahrheit singen, ist ein andrer Hauch.
Ein Hauch um nichts. Ein Wehn im Gott. Ein Wind.

BOOK I

I, 3[3]

A god can do it. Who but a god can follow
through the lute's labyrinth and not be lost?
Man's mind's in discord. Where two heart-paths cross
be sure – there stands no temple to Apollo.

For you, the song does not point towards desire,
nor promise vague, awaited, far-off bliss.
The song is being itself. A god can sing this.
But when shall *we?* When shall our being acquire

and bind unto itself the earth and stars?
This is not love, fond, callow youth,
what now bursts forth full-throated from your heart.

Forget that shriek. Its echo soon will die.
It takes a different breath to sing the truth.
Inspired by nothing. Blown through God. A sigh.

---

[3] Another motif running through these poems is the art of poetry and the vocation of the poet: to praise, to speak truth, to celebrate the wonder of being.

I, 4

O ihr Zärtlichen, tretet zuweilen
in den Atem, der euch nicht meint,
laßt ihn an eueren Wangen sich teilen,
hinter euch zittert er, wieder vereint.

O ihr Seligen, o ihr Heilen,
die ihr der Angang der Herzen scheint.
Bogen der Pfeile and Ziele von Pfeilen,
Ewiger glänzt euer Lächeln verweint.

Fürchtet euch nicht zu leiden, die Schwere,
gebt sie zurück an der Erde Gewicht;
schwer sind die Berge, schwer sind die Meere.

Selbst die als Kinder ihr pflanztet, die Bäume,
wurden zu schwer längst; ihr trüget sie nicht.
Aber die Lüfte...aber die Räume...

BOOK I

I, 4[4]

O sweet young things, sometime make your way
    out into the moment not meant for you,
    and parting over your features, let it play
    and slip beyond you, trembling, to renew

    its interrupted union. O you saved,
who stand whole, blessed, healed, at the heart's threshold,
    Bow and target, arrow's womb and grave,
    through your tears the unending smile unfolds.

    Don't fear the weight of sorrow. Let it drop
    back down into the earth, a heavy gift.
    The mountains bear down on you, and the seas,

    the trees of memory, your childhood's crop,
    soon they too will become too heavy to lift,
    but the open expanses...and the breeze...

---

[4] Perhaps a Vera poem? Or perhaps, like § 24, addressed to young people everywhere?

I, 5

Errichtet keinen Denkstein. Laßt die Rose
nur jedes Jahr zu seinen Gunsten blühn.
Denn Orpheus ists. Seine Metamorphose
in dem und dem. Wir sollen uns nicht mühn

um andre Namen. Ein für alle Male
ists Orpheus, wenn es singt. Er kommt und geht.
Ists nicht schon viel, wenn er die Rosenschale
um ein paar Tage manchmal übersteht?

O wie er schwinden muss, daß ihrs begrifft!
Und wenn ihm selbst auch bangte, daß er schwände.
In dem sein Wort das Hiersein übertrifft,

ist er schon dort, wohin ihrs nich begleitet.
Der Leier Gitter zwängt ihm nicht die Hände.
Und er gehorcht, in dem er überschreitet.

I, 5[5]

No need for a tombstone. Only ask
each year a rose breathe forth his memory.
For it is Orpheus. In whatever mask
of metamorphosis, and free

beyond all naming towards which we might strive.
Know: Orpheus lives in each song, comes and goes.
And it's a great thing if he should survive
by some few days, the petals of the rose.

Though he may vanish into his own fear,
he must leave, so that you may understand!
Just when his word meets and surpasses "here",

he's gone – to some unfollowable place.
The lute-strings can no longer tempt his hand.
At the threshold of surrender, he obeys.

---

[5] Back to Orpheus, perhaps as the archetypal poet, who transcends the everyday through art; to put it in Heideggerian terms, who rescues us from the oblivion of being.

I, 6

Ist er ein Hiesiger? Nein, aus beiden
Reichen erwuchs seine weite Natur.
Kundiger böge die Zweige der Weiden,
Wer die Würzeln der Weiden erfuhr.

Geht ihr zu Bette, so laßt auf dem Tische
Brot nicht und Milch nicht; die Toten ziehts – .
Aber er, der Beschwörende, mische
under der Milde des Augenlids

ihre Erscheinung in alles Geschaute;
und der Zauber von Erdrauch und Raute
sei ihm so wahr wie der klarste Bezug.

Nichts kann das gültige Bild ihm verschlimmern;
sei es aus Gräbern, sei es aus Zimmern,
rühme er Fingerring, Spange, und Krug.

I, 6[6]

Who is he? What is he? Where does he come from?
Not here, where the branches bend to the heath.
No – his broad nature spans the two kingdoms,
the branches which curve to the roots beneath.

To bed now, but don't leave the milk or the bread
out on the table to draw the wraiths.
Let him conjure visions, or smoothly wed
under his eyelids, their ghostly shades

in all his looking. Let it seem –
the spell of smoke and rue – a dream
of pure connection. Nothing scars

a true reflection. Whether the thing
that's praised be jug, or clasp, or ring,
neither cell nor grave can bring him harm.

---

[6] I have tried here to replicate the sound of drumming hooves that seems to pervade this sonnet; something akin to the piano accompaniment to Schubert's *Erlkönig*. This is the first of the '*Ding*' sonnets, in which Rilke breaks open mere 'things' to uncover the wonder and beauty of being revealed through apparently mundane objects.

I, 7

Rühmen, das ists! Ein zum Rühmen Bestellter,
ging er hervor wie das Erz aus des Steins
Schweigen. Sein Herz, o vergängliche Kelter
eines den Menschen unendlichen Weins.

Nie versagt ihm die Stimme am Staube,
wenn ihn das göttliche Beispiel ergreift.
Alles wird Weinberg, alles wird Traube,
in seinem fühlendem Süden gereift.

Nicht in den Grüften der Könige Moder
straft ihm die Rühmung Lügen, oder
daß von den Göttern ein Schatten fällt.

Er ist einer der bleibenden Boten,
der noch weit in die Türen der Toten
Schalen mit rühmlichen Früchten hält.

I, 7[7]

To praise is all! A tiller of praise draws forth
like ore from the stone's silence, his gold-glory.
And from the fragile wine-press of the heart pours
an infinite wine, telling the ancient story.

Even a voice come to dust shall not deny
him, when he is seized by the godlike role,
then all must turn to cluster-laden vine,
ripened in the full south of his soul.

Nor shall praise belie decay
in the vaults of the kings, or ever say
that from the gods long shadows shoot.

Immortal messenger, he shall yet
bring to the portals of the dead
bowls brimming over with mythic fruit.

---

[7] With 7, 8, and 9, we have a trilogy of poems about the poet's vocation, the singer with one foot on the earth and one in the unearthly realm.

I, 8

Nur im Raum der Rühmung darf die Klage
gehn, die Nymphe des geweinten Quells,
wachend über unserm Niederschlage,
dass er klar sei an demselben Fels,

der die Töre trägt und die Altäre. –
Sieh, um ihre stillen Schultern früht
das Gefühl, daß sie die jüngste wäre
unter den Geschwistern im Gemüt.

Jubel *weiss*, und Sehnsucht ist geständig, -
nur die Klage lernt noch; mädchenhändig
zählt sie nächtelang das alte Schlimme.

Aber plötzlich, schräg und ungeübt,
hält sie doch ein Sternbild unsrer Stimme,
in den Himmel, den ihr Hauch nicht trübt.

I, 8

And only where Praise dwells may Sorrow walk,
at the mourning spring, the guardian nymph,
keeping her watch by our precipitous fall
to see that it run clear from that same cliff

which bears both heaven's altar and heaven's gate.—
Now, blooming 'round her tranquil shoulders, see
the dawning sense that she arrived but late
to join her sister passions. It may be

Rejoicing *knows*, Desire recites her creed,
but, hands clasped, Sorrow learns the litany
of ancient woes, told through the long night hours,

when sudden from the heavens there slants down
a starburst unrehearsed, with one voice – ours –
and her sigh does not dim its shining sound.

I, 9

Nur wer die Leier schon hob
auch unter Schatten,
darf das unendliche Lob
ahnend erstatten.

Nur wer mit Toten vom Mohn
aß, von dem ihren,
wird nicht den leisesten Ton
wieder verlieren.

Mag auch die Spieglung im Teich
oft uns verschwimmen:
Wisse das Bild.

Erst in dem Doppelbereich
werden die Stimmen
ewig und mild.

I, 9

He only, whose lyre is raised
even in darkness, can bring
back the infinite praise
which he alone can sing.

He only who oft-times has shared
poppies with dead men,
never shall the slightest sound dare
to escape him again.

Though the reflection be blurred:
be sure of what oft
filled the shadow.

Then from the looking-glass world,
endless, soft
voices shall follow.

I, 10

Euch, die ihr nie mein Gefühl verließt,
grüß ich, antikische Sarkophage,
die das fröhliche Wasser römische Tage
als ein wandelndes Lied durchfließt.

Oder jene so offenen, wie das Aug
eines frohen erwachenden Hirten,
- innen voll Stille und Bienensaug –
denen entzückte Falter entschwirrten;

alle, die man dem Zweifel entreißt,
grüß ich, die wiedergeöffneten Munde,
die schon wußten, was schweigen heißt.

Wissen wirs, Freunde, wissen wirs nicht?
Beides bildet die zögernde Stunde
in dem menschlichen Angesicht.

I, 10[8]

You who in feeling have never been absent from me,
ancient sarcophagi, gladly I greet you,
as the laughing Roman waters rushed to meet you
and flow through you, in meandering melody.

Or you there, joyfully open as the eye
of an awakening shepherd – full within
of archangel and silence, still and white –
whence butterflies, enraptured, whirr and spin.

You, who are rescued now from doubt,
I greet you all, who are aware
of silence's true meaning; open mouths,

we know it well, don't we, my empty friends,
how it is the face is formed to bear
that trembling hour that holds back the end.

---

[8] This sonnet refers to some sarcophagi that also appear in *Malte Laurids Brigge*, in the ancient necropolis of Alyscamps near Arles. These were also subjects of paintings by van Gogh and Gauguin. The 'archangel' of the second stanza is another name for the wildflower Bee Nettle, also known as Dumb Nettle because it does not sting. This plant is often used in herbal remedies to reduce inflammation.

I, 11

Sieh den Himmel. Heißt kein Sternbild *Reiter*?
Den dies ist uns seltsam eingeprägt;
dieser Stolz aus Erde. Und ein Zweiter,
der ihn treibt und hält und den er trägt.

Ist nicht so, gejagt und dann gebändigt,
diese sehnige Natur des Seins?
Weg und Wendung. Doch ein Druck verständigt.
Neue Weite. Und die zwei sind eins.

Aber *sind* sie's? Oder meinen beide
nicht den Weg, den sie zusammen tun?
Namenlos schon trennt sie Tisch und Weide.

Auch die sternische Verbindung trügt.
Doch uns freue eine Weile nun
der Figur zu glauben. Das genügt.

I, 11

Search the sky. Is there no constellation
called 'the Knight'? A proud, near-earthly form
bears down on us. A second revelation
checks, drives, is farther by him borne.

Isn't it just so, overwhelmed in flight,
that being's sinewy nature is undone?
A path unfolds a turning, breaks insight
into new vistas. Suddenly, two are one.

Ah, but *are* they? Or does neither plan
to pass this way? Already a dread abyss
divides man's table from the tableland.

And though the starry union is untrue,
it pleased us for a while to think that this
unmeaning held some pattern. That must do.

I, 12

Heil dem Geist, der uns verbinden mag;
den wir leben wahrhaft in Figuren.
Und mit kleinen Schritten gehn die Uhren
neben unserm eigentlichen Tag.

Ohne unsern wahren Platz zu kennen,
handeln wir aus wirklichem Bezug.
Die Antennen fühlen die Antennen,
und die leere Ferne trug...

Reine Spannung. O Musik der Kräfte!
Ist nicht durch die läßlichen Geschäfte
jede Störung von dir abgelenkt?

Selbst wenn sich der Bauer sorgt und handelt,
wo die Saat in Sommer sich verwandelt,
reicht er niemals hin. Die Erde *schenkt*.

I, 12

Long live the spirit that may yet reveal
a plan for us midst lives but roughly sketched.
As with infinite steps, the hours stretch
forth towards our at last becoming real.

Until then we, our true place still discerning,
act as if we knew both why and when.
Our antennae not quite touching, yearning,
towards the blank distances which bear…

pure attention. Music of the spheres!
In our careless spinning of the gears
isn't each disjunction set adrift?

Even as the farmer labours, tends
the seed transformed by summer, in the end
the fruit is never his; it is earth's *gift*.

I, 13

Voller Apfel, Birne und Banane,
Stachelbeere...Alles dieses spricht
Tod und Leben in den Mund...Ich ahne...
Lest es einem Kind vom Angesicht,

Wenn es sie erschmeckt. Dies kommt von weit.
Wird euch langsam namenlos im Munde?
Wo sonst Worte waren, fließen Funde,
aus dem Fruchtfleisch überrascht befreit.

Wagt zu sagen, was ihr Apfel nennt.
Diese Süße, die sich erst verdichtet,
um, im Schmecken leise aufgerichtet,

Klar zu werden, wach und transparent,
doppeldeutig, sonnig, erdig, hiesig – ;
O Erfahrung, Fühlung, Freude – , riesig!

I, 13[9]

Full-ripened fruits, banana, pear,
gooseberry, apple... whisper to my mouth
of death and life. The tale they bear
fills me with foreboding...I read it out

on a child's face as he tastes. This came
from far beyond. And will it slowly grow,
surprised by freedom, into what can't be named?
Where once were only words, discoveries flow.

Dare to contain this sweetness now compressed
into an apple's form, within a word.
Lightly set into the taste, alert,

translucent, willing now to be expressed,
Speaking of earth, sun, *here* in twofold sense –
O joy, sensation, feeling – how immense!

---

[9] After two poems on stargazing (11 and 12), Rilke brings his gaze to the table: a poetic still life, a *'Ding'* poem.

I, 14

Wir gehen um mit Blume, Weinblatt, Frucht.
Sie sprechen nicht die Sprache nur des Jahres.
Aus Dunkel steigt ein buntes Offenbares
und hat vielleicht den Glanz der Eifersucht

der Toten an sich, die die Erde Stärken.
Was wissen wir von ihrem Teil an dem?
Es ist seit lange ihre Art, den Lehm
mit ihrem freien Marke zu durchmärken.

Nun fragt sich nur: tun sie es gern?...
Drängt diese Frucht, ein Werk von schweren Sklaven,
geballt zu uns empor, zu ihren Herrn?

Sind *sie* die Herrn, die bei den Wurzeln schlafen,
und gönnen uns aus ihren Überflüssen
dies Zwischending aus stummer Kraft und Küssen?

I, 14[10]

We are possessed by vineleaf, fruit and flower,
eloquent, in the dark, of more than time.
In them a dappled revelation shines,
that has about it the dim gleam and glower

of the jealous dead who weight the earth.
And what do we know of the part they play?
For long have they imprinted on the clay
the token of our ownership by death.

Do they will it?...Are these clusters
the work of hard-used slaves? Ask: does the fruit
force itself upwards, up to us, their masters?

Or are *these* lords, asleep among the roots,
who grant from their untold abundance this
hybrid of mute, dumb strength and silent kiss?

---

[10] Here Rilke calls into question the role of consciousness. What sort of life-force is dominant? Can we know?

I, 15

Wartet...das schmeckt...Schon ists auf der Flucht.
...Wenig Musik nur, ein Stampfen, wie in Summen – ;
Mädchen, ihr warmen, Mädchen, ihr stummen,
tanzt den Geschmack der erfahrenen Frucht!

Tanzt die Orange. Wer kann sie vergessen,
wie sie, ertrinkend in sich, sich wehrt
wider ihr Süßsein. Ihr habt sie besessen.
Sie hat sich köstlich zu euch bekehrt.

Tanzt die Orange. Die wärmere Landschaft,
werft sie aus euch, daß die reife erstrahle
in Lüften der Heimat! Erglühte, enthüllt

Düfte um Düfte. Schafft die Verwandtschaft
mit der reinen, sich weigernden Schale,
mit dem Saft, der die glückliche füllt!

I, 15[11]

Wait...that goodness...even now escapes you.
Leaving a trace of music: thrum, and beat.
Come, you maidens, in a wordless heat
dance the flavour of the tasted fruit!

Dance the orange. For who can forget
how, drowning in sweetness, it yet resists
its own sweet essence. Which you have possessed.
Which formed itself within you, exquisite.

Dance the orange. Let the ripeness stream
along the winds of home; cast that land's warmth!
Catch its fire, its fragrances unloose,

sigh on perfumed sigh. And make it seem
that you and it are one – a kin-bond form
with pure, unyielding rind, full-filling juice!

---

[11] Another '*Ding*' poem, which shows how much life can be contained within a simple object.

I, 16

Du, mein Freund, bist einsam, weil...
wir machen mit Worten und Fingerzeigen
uns allmählich die Welt zu eigen,
vielleicht ihren schwächsten, gefährlichsten Teil.

Wer zeigt mit Fingern auf einen Geruch? –
doch von den Kräften, die uns bedrohten,
fühlst du viele...Du kennst die Toten,
und du erschrickst vor dem Zauberspruch.

Sieh, nun heißt es zusammen ertragen
Stückwerk und Teile, als sei es das Ganze.
Dir helfen, wird schwer sein. Vor allem: pflanzen

mich nicht in dein Herz. Ich wüchse zu schnell.
Doch *meines* Herrn Hand will ich führen und sagen:
Hier. Das ist Esau in seinem Fell.

BOOK I

I, 16[12]

Friend, it is we who forge your loneliness...
Seeking, by word and wordless sign, to take
the world unto ourselves, perhaps to make
its breaking-point our own, most perilous.

Which of us can finger out a smell?
You feel the forces which cast threats of dread,
menacing us...well you know the dead
and start with fear at every chanted spell.

But look: now fragments as the whole must play;
we must bear brokenness. Too hard to help
you. No – don't root me in yourself.

Too soon your too-small heart would bind me in.
But I *my* master's hand will guide, and say:
Behold: Esau is here, in his own skin.

---

[12] This sonnet, of course, refers to the original story of sibling rivalry, between the twin sons of Isaac and Rebecca from Genesis 27:1 – 40. The 'master' here is Orpheus, the god of poetry.

I, 17

Zu unterst der Alte, verworrn,
all der Erbauten
Wurzel, verborgener Born,
den sie nie schauten.

Sturmhelm und Jägerhorn,
Spruch von Ergrauten,
Männer im Bruderzorn,
Frauen wie Lauten...

Drängender Zweig an Zweig,
nirgends ein freier...
Einer! O steig...o steig...

Aber sie brechen noch.
Dieser erst oben doch
beigt sich zur Leier.

I, 17

The root-stock lies hidden, concealed
under the tangles of vine,
their well-spring, never revealed,
from the beginning of time.

Helmets come forward, and horns,
the proverbs of old men,
those wroth with brotherly scorn,
and lute-figured maidens...

The branches press on, entwine,
not one can escape...
One now is climbing!...oh, climb...

But they continue to break.
Till one on high bows low, to take
form in the lyre's shape.

I, 18

Hörst du das Neue, Herr,
dröhnen und beben?
Kommen Verkündiger,
dies zu erheben.

Zwar ist kein Hören heil
in dem Durchtobtsein,
doch der Maschinenteil
will jetzt gelobt sein.

Sieh, die Maschine:
wie sie sich waltz und rächt
und uns entstellt und schwächt.

Hat sie aus uns auch Kraft,
sie, ohne Leidenschaft,
treibe und diene.

I, 18[13]

Orpheus, can you hear
what is new boom and roar?
Let prophets now appear
to pay it homage. For

Surely no hearing is safe
from violation
when mere components chafe
for veneration.

Behold the engine:
it thrashes and plunges,
displaces, wreaks vengeance,

saps all our strength, and then,
wholly indifferent,
smoothly runs on.

---

[13] This sonnet, along with I, 24 and II, 10, is a reaction against mechanization: can the ancient gods hear prayer through the noise of modern life?

I, 19

Wandelt sich rasch auch die Welt
wie Wolkengestalten,
alles Vollendete fällt
heim zum Uralten.

Über dem Wandel und Gang,
weiter und freier,
währt noch dein Vor-Gesang,
Gott mit der Leier.

Nicht sind die Leiden erkannt,
nicht ist die Liebe gelernt,
und was im Tod uns entfernt,

ist nicht entschleiert.
Einzig das Lied überm Land
heiligt und feiert.

I, 19[14]

Swift as the earth now revolves
like cloud-shapes in storm
creation, completed, devolves
back to its first form.

Above all this, your ancient song,
Lyre-god, echoes,
free and high it lingers on,
beyond all change. And although

suffering is yet a mystery,
and love has not yet been learned,
and we have yet to discern

how life in death is withdrawn,
alone over all, making holy
and whole, floats your song.

---

[14] Sonnets 19, 20, and 21 address Orpheus directly. In the notes which accompany the first printing of the Sonnets, Rilke says of I, 21: 'The little 'Spring Melody' seems have the same structure as a remarkably dancelike tune which I once heard the pupils sing at a morning mass in the convent church in Ronda (in southern Spain). The children sang a text with which I was unfamiliar to a dance rhythm, accompanied with triangle and tambourine.'

I, 20

Dir aber, Herr, o was weih ich dir, sag,
der das Ohr den Geschöpfen gelehrt? –
Mein Erinnern an einen Frühlingstag,
seinen Abend, in Rußland – , ein Pferd...

Herüber vom Dorf kam der Schimmel allein,
an der vorderen Fessel den Pflock,
um die Nacht auf den Wiesen allein zu sein;
wie schlug seiner Mähne Gelock

an den Hals im Takte des Übermuts,
bei dem grob gehemmten Galopp.
Wie sprangen die Quellen des Rossebluts!

Der fühlte die Weiten, und ob!
Der sang und der hörte – , dein Sagenkreis
war *in* ihm geschlossen.
Sein Bild: ich weih's.

I, 20

Say, Lord, what offering could I bring
to you who opened the ear, taught sound
to creation? Memory holds a Russian spring
at evening – , a horse's hooves that pound

in from the village. Alone he came,
a white horse, forelegs hobbled, to pass
the night alone on high ground. Without shame,
in a proud rhythm tossed

high the flowing waves of his mane,
defying his crudely fettered gait,
a charger's blood rushing in his veins!

Scenting horizons – away!
The image as he sang, stilled – , enfolding
your legend *within* him:
this I bring.

I, 21

Frühling ist wiedergekommen. Die Erde
ist wie win Kind, das Gedichte weiβ;
viele, o viele...Für die Beschwerde
langen Lernens bekommt sie den Preis.

Streng war ihr Lehrer. Wir mochten das Weiβe
an dem Barte des alten Manns.
Nun, wie das Grüne, das Blaue heiβe,
dürfen wir fragen: sie kanns, sie kanns!

Erde, die frei hat, du glückliche, spiele
nun mit den Kindern. Wir wollen dich fange,
fröhliche Erde. Dem Frohsten gelingts.

O, was der Lehrer sie lehrte, das Viele,
und was gedruckt steht in Wurzeln und langen
schwierigen Stämmen: sie singts, sie singts.

I, 21

So spring is come again. The earth
once more is like a child so wise
who holds, oh, so many poems within her
and for her pains receives the prize.

She had a strict teacher. How fond we've been
of the white of that old man's beard. Just ask
her now to tell what's blue, what green:
she knows it, that's an easy task!

Play, Earth, in your happy leisure,
now with these little ones. You're it, come on,
glad earth. Who laughs truest, wins.

How much that teacher taught her – the measure
of music hidden in reeds, in long,
tough roots: just listen to her sing!

I, 22

Wir sind die Treibenden.
Aber den Schritt der Zeit,
nehmt ihn als Kleinigkeit
im immer Bleibenden.

Alles das Eilende
wird schon vorüber sein;
denn das Verweilende
erst weiht uns ein.

Knaben, o werft den Mut
nicht in die Schnelligkeit,
nicht in den Flugversuch.

Alles ist ausgeruht:
Dunkel und Helligkeit,
Blume und Buch.

BOOK I

I, 22[15]

We drive life on. Yet see
Time's span as just a bagatelle,
tiny, infinitesimal
in the vastness of eternity.

And know: when all that rushes past
shall long be done, gone beyond haste,
only then shall that which lasts
welcome us as initiates.

Oh my sweet youths, don't cast
your strength away on speed,
the mere pursuit of flight.

All this shall come to rest:
the flower, this book you read,
the dark, the bright.

---

[15] The subject shifts back here to the 'youth' addressed in § 4.

I, 23

O erst *dann*, wenn der Flug
nicht mehr um seinetwillen
wird in die Himmelstillen
steigen, sich selber genug,

um in lichten Profilen,
als das Gerät, das gelang,
Liebling der Winde zu spielen,
sicher schwenkend und schlank, -

erst wenn ein reines Wohin
wachsender Apparate
Knabenstolz überwiegt,

wird, überstürzt von Gewinn,
jener den Fernen Genahte
sein, was er einsam erfliegt.

I, 23

Then, oh *then*, when flight
rises for the first time heeding
itself no more, and needing
only that, rises to the height

of heaven's stillness, and appears
in silhouette, at last become
a plaything for the zephyrs,
lithe and supple, – it shall have won,

for the first time, over pride, –
when at last direction
builds, then one who was far off

shall draw close, nearly toppled by the tide
of its success, and in perfection
be, and lonely, soar aloft.

I, 24

Sollen wir unsere Freundschaft, die großen
niemals werbenden Götter, weil sie der harte
Stahl, den wir streng erzogen, nicht kennt, verstoßen
oder sie plötzlich suchen auf einer Karte?

Diese gewaltigen Freunde, die uns die Toten
nehmen, rühren nirgends an unsere Räder.
Unsere Gastmähler haben wir weit −, unsere Bäder,
fortgerückt, und ihre uns lang schon zu langsamen Boten

überholen wir immer. Einsamer nun auf einander
ganz angewiesen, ohne einander zu kennen,
führen wir nicht mehr die Pfade als schone Mäander,

sondern als Grade. Nur noch in Dampfkesseln brennen
die einstigen Feuer und heben die Hämmer, die immer
größern. Wir aber nehmen an Kraft ab, wie Schwimmer.

I, 24[16]

Since we no longer pray, shall we forsake
our erstwhile friends, the gods – who disregard
our great, hard-won achievements? Shall we take
their final secrets from them? It seems hard

those mighty friends who still receive our dead
no longer touch us. Now our feasts take place,
as do our purifying rites, a great way off, and we've outpaced
long since their heralds. We are isolated,

lonelier now, estranged, by all bereft.
We wander paths no more, but advance by degrees.
The final relic of Prometheus' theft

now stokes a boiler, Hephaestos' hammer breeds
pistons now. All the while, amidst these clamours,
we sink, dispirited, like weary swimmers.

---

[16] Here I admit that I took a liberty and inserted an image that Rilke only hints at: while he is clearly thinking of ancient Greek mythology, he makes no explicit mention of Prometheus and Hephaistos. *Mea culpa*.

I, 25

Dich aber will ich nun, *Dich*, die ich kannte
wie eine Blume, von der ich den Namen nicht weiß,
noch ein Mal erinnern und ihnen zeigen, Entwandte,
Schöne Gespielin des unüberwindlichen Schrei's.

Tänzerin erst, die plötzlich, den Körper voll Zögern,
anhielt, als göß man ihr Jungsein in Erz;
trauernd und lauschend -. Da, von den hohen Vermögern
fiel ihr Musik in das veränderte Herz.

Nah war die Krankheit. Schon von den Schatten bemächtigt,
drängte verdunkelt das Blut, doch, wie flüchtig verdächtigt,
trieb es in seinen natürlichen Frühling hervor.

Wieder und wieder, von Dunkel und Sturz unterbrochen,
glänzte es irdisch. Bis es nach schrecklichem Pochen
trat in das trostlos offene Tor.

I, 25[17]

It's *you* that I want to remember now,
to show them, *you* – who long since have stolen away
nameless, whom I only sensed, as one senses a flower –
gone forever the shout of your laughter in play.

At first she danced. Of a sudden, her body went taut,
as though her youth were cast in bronze; as hearkening
to a silent cry, or mourning some lost
joy; and music struck her heart. Darkening,

the blood raced through her veins as though fleeing suspicion,
possessed by phantoms; in its relentless progression
Death loomed. And the sickness drove on.

Life faltered, flashed as darkness plunged, swept
over her, till with one great thrill she stepped
past hope, through the welcoming door, and was gone.

---

[17] This poem outlines Vera's attempts to continue an artistic life over the course of her illness.

I, 26

Du aber, Göttlicher, du, bis zuletzt noch Ertöner,
da ihn der Schwarm der verschmähten Mänaden befiel,
hast ihr Geschrei übertönt mit Ordnung, du Schöner,
aus den Zerstörenden stieg dein erbauendes Spiel.

Keine war da, daß sie Haupt dir und Leier zerstör.
Wie sie auch rangen und rasten, und alle die scharfen
Steine, die sie nach deinem Herzen warfen,
wurden zu Sanftem an dir und begabt mit Gehör.

Schließlich zerschlugen sie dich, vor der Rache gehetzt,
während dein Klang noch in Löwen und Felsen verweilte
und in den Bäumen und Vögeln. Dort singst du noch jetzt.

O du verlorener Gott! Du unendliche Spur!
Nur weil dich reißend zuletzt die Feindschaft verteilte,
sind wir die Hörenden jetzt und ein Mund der Natur.

BOOK I

I, 26[18]

But God, right up until the last you sang,
    as they fell, rejected furies, in a throng
upon you. Above their cries, your calm tone rang
    out lovely, from the ruins, your uplifting song.

Not one was there could crush your head, your lyre,
    however they struggled and raved – and all the sharp
    stones, hurled from hatred at your heart,
grew soft, began to hear. At last, on fire

with rage, they tore you asunder, the while your ringing
    tones yet lingered in the birds, in trees,
    in cliffs, in beasts. There even now you sing.

    Forsaken god! By hatred rendered out
    to all – Oh infinite echo's wake – that we
    might hear you now, from Nature's mouth.

---

[18] The first book closes with an image from the final 'moment' of the Orpheus myth.

Book II

II, 1

Atmen, du unsichtbares Gedicht!
Immerfort um das eigne
sein rein eingetauschter Weltraum, Gegengewicht,
in dem ich mich rhythmisch ereigne.

Einige Welle, deren
allmähliches Meer ich bin;
sparsamstes du von allen möglichen Meeren, –
Raumgewinn.

Wieviele von diesen Stellen der Räume waren schon
innen in mir. Manche Winde
sind wie mein Sohn.

Erkennst du mich, Luft, du, voll noch einst meiniger Orte?
Du, einmal glatte Rinde,
Rundung und Blatt meiner Worte.

II, 1[19]

Breath, invisible poem! A ceaseless
flow renews your life,
A pure exchange of inner, outer space.
Pendulum, in whose rhythm I rise

From out a single wave,
that builds into my sea;
culling from every possible sea some space,
you create infinity.

A vastness – of whose stars how many already shone within me.
Sometimes like a child, a son,
a breeze moves through me.

Do you, breath of my home, still feel me stir
within you? You, who once
formed the curve and leaf and smooth flesh of my words?

---

[19] In this first poem of Book II, the mystery of breath is explored. What is breath, after all? Rilke invites us to reconsider the most natural, indispensable and unexamined aspect of our lives.

II, 2

So wie dem Meister manchmal das eilig
nähere Blatt den *wirklichen* Strich
abnimmt; so nehmen oft Spiegel das heilig
einzige Lächeln der Mädchen in sich,

wenn sie den Morgen erproben, allein –
oder im Glanze der dienenden Lichter.
Und in das Atmen der echten Gesichter,
später, fällt nur ein Widerschein.

Was haben Augen einst ins umrußte
lange Verglühn der Kamine geschaut:
Blicke des Lebens, für immer verlorne.

Ach, der Erde, wer kennt die Verluste?
Nur, wer mit dennoch preisenden Laut
sange das Herz, das ins Ganze geborne.

II, 2[20]

Just as it sometimes chances that, snatching
the nearest scrap to sketch a thought,
the master completes it — just so, catching
a glimpse of a girl as she ventures out

alone in the morning — or her chaste,
exquisite smile in the gleam of the lamplight —
mirrors often cast back what is not yet in sight:
the reflection of being, the true face.

What *was* it glimmered in the fire
slowly cooling in the hearth?
A glint of life, forever lost.

Only the poet, who with his lyre
can praise the ever-renewing heart,
can sing earth's pain. Can count the cost.

---

[20] Here Rilke seems to suggest that the elusive essence of human being can only be articulated in poetry, if at all.

II, 3

Spiegel: noch nie hat man wissend beschrieben
was ihr in euerem Wesen seid.
Ihr, wie mit lauter Löchern von Sieben
erfüllten Zwischenräume der Zeit.

Ihr, noch des leeren Saales Verschwender –,
Wenn es dämmert, wie Wälder weit...
Under der Lüster geht wie ein Sechzehn-Ender
durch eure Unbetretbarkeit.

Manchmal seid ihr voll Malerei.
Einige scheinen *in* euch gegangen – ,
andere schicktet ihr scheu vorbei.

Aber die Schönste wird bleiben, bis
drüben in ihre enthaltenen Wangen
eindrang der klare gelöste Narziß.

II, 3[21]

Mirrors: no one has yet explained
your essential nature, reckoned
how, porous as sieves, you yet contain
the intervals between each second.

Like depthless forests at twilight, in vacant
rooms – you are wantonly empty.
Like a sixteen-pointed stag, huge, ancient,
a breeze can pierce your destiny.

Sometimes painters try to fill you;
while some skirt round you with bashful images,
others seem to have stepped right *through*.

But the last, most beautiful will remain,
until within your imprisoning visage is
discovered: Narcissus, past all pain.

---

[21] The stag referred to here was most likely a hunting trophy. As they grow (up to the age of ten or so), deers' antlers become increasingly fuller. A mature stag would have anywhere from 12 – 30 points or branches. In hunting parlance, a sixteen-pointed stag is called a Monarch.

II, 4

O dieses ist das Tier, das es nicht gibt.
Sie wußtens nicht und habens jeden Falls
– sein Wandeln, seine Haltung, seinen Hals,
bis in des stillen Blickes Licht – geliebt.

Zwar *war* es nicht. Doch weil sie's liebten, ward
ein reines Tier. Sie ließen immer Raum.
Und in dem Raume, klar und ausgespart,
erhob es leicht sein Haupt und brauchte kaum

zu sein. Sie nährten es mit keinem Korn,
nur immer mit der Möglichkeit, es sei.
Und die gab solche Stärke an das Tier,

daß es aus sich ein Stirnhorn trieb. Ein Horn.
Zu einer Jungfrau kam es weiss herbei –
und war in Silber-Spiegel und in ihr.

II, 4[22]

Ah, here is the creature that only exists in myth.
Unknown, and most likely – unless of a sudden, seen
in a still flash of inspiration – unloved, with
its changeling form, its lovely neck and bearing.

At least – it *didn't* exist. But while they loved it,
and because they did, the creature *was*.
They gave it sanctuary. There it lifted
up its graceful head and needed just

to be. They fed it, not on grain, but on
the possibility of being. Quite
inspired, drawn onward by that hope, it flowered,

putting forth a horn. Just one. And shone,
in keeping with her pureness, white,
and lives on in the mirror, and her heart.

---

[22] This poem seems to refer to the famous medieval tapestry of 'The Lady and the Unicorn', reproductions of which graced many European villas.

II, 5

Blumenmuskel, der der Anemone
Wiesenmorgen nach und nach erschließt,
bis in ihren Schooß das polyphone
Licht der lauten Himmel sich ergießt,

In den stillen Blütenstern gespannter
Muskel des unendlichen Empfangs,
manchmal *so* von Fülle übermannter
daß der Ruhewink des Untergangs

kaum vermag die weitzurück geschnellten
Blätterränder dir zurückzugeben:
du, Entschluß und Kraft von *wie*viel Welten!

Wir, Gewaltsamen, wir währen länger.
Aber *wann*, in welchem aller Leben,
sind wir endlich offen und Empfänger?

II, 5[23]

Your muscles furled, anemone,
open, flex in the dawnfields, til
washed over by the polyphony
of Heaven's light, gushing into the still

heart of the flower of your womb,
the tensed muscles of infinite reception,
sometimes by fullness *so* overcome
that the hushing gesture of the setting sun

can scarcely make the rippling leaf-crests
return, surrender themselves again:
serene and steadfast strength of countless

worlds! By force, we will outlast you.
But *when*, in which life – among how many –
will we open at last, to receive as you do?

---

[23] This begins three poems about flowers.

II, 6

Rose, du tronende, denen in Altertume
warst du ein Kelch mit einfachem Rand.
Uns aber bist du die volle zahllose Blume,
der unerschöpfliche Gegenstand.

In deinem Reichtum scheinst du wie Kleidung um Kleidung
um einen Leib aus nichts als Glanz;
aber dein einzelnes Blatt ist zugleich die Vermeidung
und die Verleugnung jedes Gewands.

Seit Jahrhunderten ruft uns dein Duft
sein süßesten Name herüber;
plötzlich liegt er wie Ruhm in der Luft.

Dennoch, wir wissen ihn nicht zu nennen, wir raten...
Und Erinnerungen geht zu ihm uber,
die wir von rufbaren Stunden erbaten.

II, 6

O rose, enthroned: to those in days of old,
you were just a chalice of simple lines.
But to *us* your countless petals enfold
an infinitely complex design.

You are robed in abundance, in layer on shimmering layer
of nothing but light. Yet your every leaf
spurns the suggestion that you should wear
any raiment. While your sweet

perfume, drifting down through time,
whispers a delicious, sudden
glory on the wind: your name,

barely felt. We cannot say it...hesitate...
it eludes us. Til memories stream forth, flood
at our bidding, from the hours where they wait.

II, 7

Blumen, ihr schließlich den ordendnen Händen verwandte,
(Händen der Mädchen von einst und jetzt),
die auf dem Gartentisch oft von Kante zu Kante
lagen, ermattet und sanft verletzt,

wartend des Wassers, das sie noch einmal erhole
aus dem begonnenen Tod – , und nun
wieder erhobene zwischen die strömenden Pole
fühlender Finger, die wohlzutun

mehr noch vermögen, als ihr ahntes, ihr leichten,
wenn ihr euch wiederfandet im Krug,
langsam erkühlend und Warmes der Mädchen, wie Beichten,

von euch gebend, wie trübe ermüdende Sünden,
die das Gepflücktsein beging, als Bezug
wieder zu ihnen, die sich euch blühend verbünden.

II, 7

Flowers: after all in said and done,
you and they – the hands of those
young girls (of any age and time) – are one;
the busy hands which once bestrewed

the garden table end to end
with you, languishing and softly bruised,
waiting for water to bring you back again
from the death already rising in you,

the radiant shafts of whose sensitive fingers lifted
you (more healing than they knew)
tenderly in to the vase, as your warmth shifted,

cooled into a dim weary memory, as of sins confessed,
as you began the life of the newly-gathered, who,
blooming, were bound to you in that caress.

II, 8
In memoriam Egon von Rilke (Malte)

Wenige ihr, der einstigen Kindheit Gespielen
in den zerstreuten Gärten der Stadt:
wie wir uns fanden und uns zögernd gefielen
und, wie das Lamm mit dem redenden Blatt,

sprachen als Schweigende. Wenn wir uns einmal freuten,
keinem gehörte es. Wessen wars?
Und wie zergings unter allen den gehenden Leuten
und im Bangen des langen Jahrs.

Wagen umrollten uns fremd, vorübergezogen,
Häuser umstanden uns stark, aber unwahr, – und keines
kannte uns je. *Was* war wirklich im All?

Nichts. Nur die Bälle. Ihre herrlichen Bogen.
Auch nicht die Kinder...aber manchmal trat eines,
ach ein vergehendes, unter den fallenden Ball.

BOOK II

II, 8[24]
In memoriam Egon von Rilke (Malte)

There were a few of us, midst those who played
hide-and-seek in the gardens of long ago,
as we frolicked through those scattered parks, and lazed
through childhood, a few like the lamb with his scroll,

whose silence spoke volumes. If we were glad,
still, no one owned the joy. Whose was it?
It melted in the ever-passing crowd,
lost in the dread of the long year's transit.

Strange vehicles rumbled by, houses surrounded us, sturdy
yet somehow unreal, – no one knew we existed.
But what really *was*, there under the eye of the All?

Nothing. Perhaps a ball. Not the children...though every
now and then, one – ah, one of those now dead –
stepped into the glorious arc of its fall.

---

[24] This poem is dedicated to a cousin of Rilke's, Egon von Rilke, who died in childhood. The 'lamb with a scroll' is another allusion to tapestries; the lamb, frequently a symbol of Christ or innocence, often 'holds' a scroll in the cleft of its hoof, on which a message is inscribed.

II, 9

Rühmt euch, ihr Richtenden, nicht der entbehrlichen Folter
    und daß das Eisen nicht länger an Hälsen sperrt,
Keins ist gesteigert, kein Herz – , weil ein gewollter
    Krampf der Milde euch zarter verzerrt.

Was es durch Zeiten bekam, das schenkt das Schafott
    wieder zurück, wie Kinder ihr Spielzeug vom vorig
    alten Geburtstag. Ins reine, ins hohe, ins torig
    offene Herz träte er enders, der Gott

wirkliche Milde. Er käme gewaltig und griffe
    stralhender um sich, wie Göttliche sind.
    Mehr als ein Wind für die großen gesicherten Schiffe.

Weniger nicht, als die heimliche leise Gewahrung,
    die uns im Innern schweigend gewinnt
    wie ein still spielendes Kind aus unendlicher Paarung.

II, 9

You who seek to judge: don't tell us now
about your needless torture, boasting how
the iron band no longer grips your throat.
None, not one heart, by the mercy that smote

your brow, was lifted. No, the scaffold tosses
back what it receives, like a child who's done
with last year's toy. The god, the gracious one,
enters each heart as it can receive him: valorous,

pure, or arching open. Let him appear
god-like, the radiance round him showing
might, a greater force than strong ships fear.

The true god comes in silence, awareness grows subtly,
in secret gives birth to an inward knowing,
like the tranquilly playing child of an infinite coupling.

II, 10

Alles Erworbne bedroht die Maschine, solange
wie sich erdreistet, im Geist, statt im Gehorchen, zu sein.
Daß nicht der herrlichen Hand schöneres Zögern mehr prange,
zu dem entschlossenern Bau schneidet sie steifer den Stein.

Nirgends bleibt sie zurück, dass wir ihr *ein* Mal entrönnen
und sie in stiller Fabrik ölend sich selber gehört.
Sie ist das Leben, – sie meint es am besten zu können,
die mit dem gleichen Entschluß ordnet und schafft und zerstört.

Aber noch ist uns das Dasein verzaubert; an hundert
Stellen ist es noch Ursprung. Ein Spielen von reinen
Kräften, die keiner berührt, der nicht kniet und bewundert.

Worte gehen noch zart am Unsäglichen aus...
Und die Musik, immer neu, aus den bebendsten Steinen,
baut im unbrauchbaren Raum ihr vergöttlichtes Haus.

II, 10[25]

Everything, every thing that has been gained,
is imperiled by the machine's conceit: that it now lives,
endowed with spirit, servile no longer. That the hand
of a master may not be displayed, still lingering, it rives

the stone more precisely, to the more rigid plan. No exit
is left us, through which to flee its oily presence, escape,
leave it to the deserted mill. Now *it* knows best,
runs *us*: one stroke creates, shapes and obliterates.

But for us, what lives and breathes is still
enchanted. In a hundred places now begins
a dazzling scene – pure power – moving all to kneel

in wonder. Frail words falter against what can't be named...
But music, every renewing, continues to raise her pagan
shrine of singing stones, in barren space.

---

[25] Here again we see Rilke struggling with the increasing mechanization of modern life. It is a thought-provoking exercise to read these sonnets against the backdrop of such essays as Heidegger's *The Question Concerning Technology* and Walter Benjamin's *The Work of Art in the Age of Mechanical Reproduction*.

II, 11

Manche, des Todes, entstand ruhig geordnete Regel,
weiterbezwingender Mensch, seit du im Jagen beharrst;
mehr doch als Falle und Netz, weiß ich dich, Streifen von Segel,
den man hinuntergehängt in den höhligen Karst.

Leise ließ man dich ein, als wärst du ein Zeichen,
Frieden zu feiern. Doch dann: rang dich am Rande der Knecht,
und, aus den Höhlen, die Nacht warf eine Handvoll von bleichen
taumelnden Tauben ins Licht…Aber auch *das* ist im Recht.

Fern von dem Schauenden sei jeglicher Hauch des Bedauerns,
nicht nur vom Jäger allein, der, was sich zeitig erweist,
wachsam und handelnd vollzieht.

Töten ist eine Gestalt unseres wandernden Trauerns…
Rein ist im heiteren Geist,
was an uns selber geschieht.

II, 11[26]

Since you persist in hunting, you will learn that death
has formed many a sober canon. Hunter, hard-driven,
you too shall fall. I know, better than any trap or net,
your wings like tattered sails, hanging in barren

caves in the karst. A sign always read easily, seeming
to promise peace. The foe wrestled you right to the edge; just then
out of the caves, the night flung a handful of pale doves careening
into the light...But even that was well. Send

now, not only from the hunter but the crowd, any ache
of regret, from the one who proved himself ready, found
himself completed in the act.

Killing is just one shape our errant sadness takes...
Purity in a quiet soul abounds,
whatever comes to pass.

---

[26] The imagery in this sonnet comes from a method of hunting small birds in a karst (a limestone cave region, such as is found, for example, in Slovenia). White strips of cloth are lowered into the caves where the birds roost. When the hunters are in place, the cloths are shaken, the birds become frightened and disoriented, and flee the caves *en masse.*

II, 12

Wolle die Wandlung. O sei für die Flamme begeistert,
Drin sich ein Ding dir entzieht, das mit Verwandlungen prunkt;
jener entwerfende Geist, welcher das Irdische meistert,
liebt in dem Schwung der Figur nichts wie den wendenden Punkt.

Was sich ins Bleiben verschließt, schon *ists* das Erstarrte;
wähnt es sich sicher im Schutz des unscheinbaren Grau's?
Warte, ein Härtestes warnt aus der Ferne das Harte.
Wehe – : abwesender Hammer holt aus!

Wer sich als Quelle ergießt, den erkennt die Erkennung;
und sie führt ihn entzückt durch das heiter Geschaffne,
das mit Anfang oft schließt und mit Ende beginnt.

Jeder glückliche Raum ist Kind oder Enkel von Trennung,
den sie staunend durchgehn. Und die verwandelte Daphne
will, seit sie lorbeern fühlt, daß du dich wandelst in Wind.

BOOK II

II, 12[27]

Long ardently to be transformed. Die with desire
for the flame in which change, elusive, proudly burns.
By the world subdued, each finds in the dancer's
swirl nothing so lovely as the point of its turn.

What wraps itself in permanence petrifies.
Does it think itself safer there, shrouded so? Just wait –
one hard thing drives another, a hammer strikes
from nowhere – woe to the one who meets that fate!

He who offers himself to flow as a wellspring knows Wisdom;
she leads him through a lovely land, enraptured,
where openings often end, endings begin;

each opening the happy offspring of division,
dashed through in wonder. While Daphne, to laurel transfigured,
her branches emerging, wants you to turn to wind.

---

[27] 12 and 13 are two of the best-known poems of this cycle. These sonnets bring to the fore one of Rilke's favourite themes, both in this cycle and throughout his work: spiritual transformation through aesthetic contemplation (a concept familiar to Schopenhauer and Nietzsche). In II, 12, Rilke calls on the Greek myth of Daphne, a river nymph who, to escape pursuit by Apollo, was transformed into a laurel bush. In her memory, a heartbroken Apollo made the evergreen laurel wreath the symbol of tribute to poets. One can also hear an echo of sorrow for Vera, the dancer.

II, 13

Sei allem Abschied voran, als wäre er hinter
dir, wie der Winter, der eben geht.
Denn unter Wintern is einer so endlos Winter,
daß, überwinternd, dein Herz überhaupt übersteht.

Sei immer tot in Eurydike – , singender steige,
preisender steige zurück in den reinen Bezug.
Hier unter Schwindenden, sei, im Reiche der Neige,
sei ein klingendes Glas, das sich im Klang schon zerschlug.

Sei – und wisse zugleich des Nicht-Seins Bedingung,
den unendlichen Grund deiner innigen Schwingung,
daß du sie völlig vollziehst dieses einzige Mal.

Zu dem gebrauchten sowohl, wie zum dumpfen und stummen
Vorrat der vollen Natur, den unsäglichen Summen,
zähle dich jubelnd hinzu und vernichte die Zahl.

II, 13[28]

Step past all parting, as if it lay already far
behind you, like the winter that is gone.
Beneath, an endless winter of the heart
enfolded you, must now be overcome.

In Eurydice be ever dead – , and in her, rise,
rise singing, back to pure love, praising. Be
here among sinking shades, a ringing glass
that shatters as it sounds. Be all this, be –

and in one matchless instant know
the perpetual pull, the inner surge and flow
of being and nothing – their union consummate.

Now: add yourself with joy to Nature's store,
to the incalculable, muffled, mute and worn,
and making up the sum, wipe clean the slate.

---

[28] Sonnet II, 13 revisits the theme of transformation through loss sublimated in aesthetic contemplation. What is most striking here for those of a philosophic bent is the idea of the union of 'being and nothing', and how these forces meet in human being.

II, 14

Siehe die Blumen, diese dem Irdischen treuen,
denen wir Schicksal vom Rande des Schicksals leihn, –
aber wer weiß es! Wenn sie ihr Welken bereuen,
ist es an uns, ihre Reue zu sein.

Alles will schweben. Da gehn wir umher wie Beschwerer,
legen auf alles uns selbst, vom Gewichte entzückt;
o was sind wir den Dingen für zehrende Lehrer,
weil ihnen ewige Kindheit glückt.

Nahme sie einer ins innige Schlagen und schliefe
tief mit den Dingen – ; o wie käme er leicht,
anders zum anderen Tag, aus der gemainsamen Tiefe.

Oder er bliebe vielleicht; und sie blühten und priesen
ihn, den Bekehrten, der nun den Ihrigen gleicht,
allen den stillen Geschwistern im Winde der Wiesen.

II, 14[29]

Look at these flowers, who vow themselves to the earth:
from destiny's rim, we lend them a fate,
but who knows if they mourn the corruption that starts at their birth?
It is we who bear the sorrow of their decay.

By nature all things float, but like ballasters, we,
charmed by mass, plod around encumbering
all with self. What spoilers we must seem
to them, in their endless childhood dream.

Let them take one with them down into that inmost sleep, –
how easily he would drift one day to the next
in that depth of oneness. He could stay in the deep

and they would bloom around him, exalting in
their newest convert, now one with the rest
of the silent brethren in the meadow wind.

---

[29] Another flower poem, in which Rilke somewhat wistfully contrasts the simple existence of flowers with overburdened human consciousness.

II, 15

O Brunnen-Mund, du gebender, du Mund,
der unerschöpflich Eines, Reines, spricht, –
du vor des Wassers fließendem Gesicht,
marmorne Maske. Und im Hintergrund

der Aquädukte Herkunft. Weither an
Gräbern vorbei, vom Hang des Apennins
tragen sie dir dein Sagen zu, das dann
am schwarzen Altern deines Kinns

vorüberfällt in das Gefäß davor.
Dies ist das schlafend hingelegte Ohr,
das Marmorohr, in das du immer sprichst.

Ein Ohr der Erde. Nur mit sich allein
redet sie also. Schiebt ein Krug sich ein,
so scheint es ihr, daß du sie unterbrichst.

II, 15[30]

Oh, old man of the fountains, your generous mouth
pours forth one tale, without change, without end, –
the rippling water's fluid face is hidden
behind your marble mask. In the background, now

the spring of the aqueduct. On streams from afar,
right past the tombs, from the distant Apennine hills
you carry your report. Then, past the marks
which age has blackened on your chin, it spills

into the channels of what lies sleeping here,
stretched out awaiting you, the marble ear,
Earth's own. And so through you she carries on

her inner discourse. And if a jug is thrust
under the spout, it only seems to interrupt
the whispering flow of the infinite conversation.

---

[30] This 'Ding' poem was most likely inspired by a feature in the gardens of Duino.

II, 16

Immer wieder von uns aufgerissen,
ist der Gott die Stelle, welche heilt.
Wir sind Scharfe, den wir wollen wissen,
aber er ist heiter und verteilt.

Selbst die reine, die geweihte Spende
nimmt er anders nicht in seine Welt,
als indem er sich dem freien Ende
unbewegt entgegenstellt.

Nur der Tote trinkt
aus der hier von uns *gehörten* Quelle,
wenn der Gott ihm schweigent winkt, dem Toten.

Uns wird nur das Lärmen angeboten.
Und das Lamm erbittet seine Schelle
aus dem stilleren Instinkt.

II, 16

Over and over again, we tear him apart,
yet the god is still the place of healing. While
driven to know, we are focused, hard.
He is in fragments, yet his heart is light.

Even the pure, the consecrated gift,
the gift of his very life, in his world's eye
is but a simple fact: that he meets death
unmoved; confronts it, and he does not die.

Only those who've heard death's knell,
if silently bidden by the god may drink
from his fountain. To *us*, though we can *hear*

the rushing spring, he offers only tears,
while the lamb, from some mute instinct,
pleads for his collar and his bell.

II, 17

Wo, in welchen immer selig bewässerten Gärten, an welchen
Bäumen, aus welchen zärtlich entblätterten Blüten-Kelchen
reifen die fremdartigen Früchte der Tröstung? Diese
köstlichen, deren du eine vielleicht in der zertretenen Wiese

deiner Armut findest. Von einem zum anderen Male
wunderst du dich über die Größe der Frucht,
über ihr Heilsein, über die Sanftheit der Schale,
und daß sie der Leichtsinn des Vogels dir nicht vorwegnahm
und nicht die Eifersucht

unten des Wurms. Gibt es denn Bäume, von Engeln beflogen,
und von verborgenen langsamen Gärtnern so seltsam gezogen,
daß sie uns tragen, ohne uns zu gehören?

Haben wir niemals vermocht, wir Schatten und Schemen,
durch unser voreilig reifes und wieder welkes Benehmen
jener gelassenen Sommer Gleichmut zu stören?

II, 17

Tell me, in which of the gardens with water blessed,
on which trees, in the chalice of which flower,
gently stripped of leaves, does the rare fruit of solace
ripen? Precious fruit which you, perhaps,
in the well-trampled fields of your

poverty may find. From time to time
you may marvel at the size, the soundness of the fruit,
the softness of its skin, and gladly find
it a wonder that neither heedless birds
nor jealous worms have stolen it from you.

Do you think there are trees over which angels bend,
so seldom gleaned by those slow unseen gardeners who tend
them, that they yield for us, although they are not ours?

We shadows and ghosts, were we never able, in the course
of our too-hasty ripening and fading, to shake by force
the placid equanimity of a summer hour?

II, 18

Tänzerin: o du Verlegung
alles Vergehens in Gang: wie brachtest du's dar.
Und der Wirbel am Schluß, dieser Baum aus Bewegung,
nahm er nicht ganz in Besitz das erschwungene Jahr?

Blühte nicht, daß ihn dein Schwingen von vorhin umschwärme,
plötzlich sein Wipfel von Stille? Und über ihr,
war sie nicht Sonne, war sie nicht Sommer, die Wärme,
dies unzählige Wärme aus dir?

Aber er trug auch, er trug, dein Baum der Ekstase.
Sind sie nicht seine ruhigen Früchte: der Krug,
reifend gestreift, und die gereifterte Vase?

Und in den Bildern: ist nicht die Zeichnung geblieben,
die deiner Braue dunkler Zug
rasch an die Wandung der eignene Wendung geschrieben?

II, 18[31]

Sweet dancer, for a while your pose
held death at a distance: grace became a prayer.
In your last whirl a tree arose,
a tree of movement, gathering hard-won years

blazing into a peak of stillness, coming
from out the swarming swelling as you turned,
and over all it was your sun, your summering,
your immeasurable heat that burned.

And yes, your tree of rapture bore fruit, bore
the fluted vase, clay pitcher: these now
are its quiet fruits. But among them one more

vivid image: is there not still a mark,
inscribed in air, the contour of your brow,
the coil and wheeling of its final torque?

---

[31] Another paean to Vera.

II, 19

Irgendwo wohnt das Gold in der verwöhnenden Bank
und mit Tausenden tut es vertraulich. Doch jener
Blinde, der Bettler, ist selbst dem kupfernen Zehner
wie ein verlorener Ort, wie das staubige Eck unterm Schrank.

In den Geschäften entlang ist das Geld wie zuhause
und verkleidet sich scheinbar in Seide, Nelken, und Pelz.
Er, der Schweigende, steht in der Atempause
alles des wach oder schlafend atmenden Gelds.

O wie mag sie sich schließen bei Nacht, diese immer offene Hand.
Morgen holt sie das Schicksal wieder, und täglich
hält es sie hin: hell, elend, unendlich zerstörbar.

Daß doch einer, ein Schauender, endlich ihren langen Bestand
staunend begriffe und rühmte. Nur dem Aufsingendem säglich.
Nur dem Göttlichen hörbar.

II, 19[32]

In some far-off vault gold has its pampered dwelling,
intimate with thousands. But a blind beggar's pocket,
to a copper coin, is just as desolate
a place as a closet's dusty underbelly.

At ease in every shop that lines the square,
in furs, carnations, silks, money tricks itself out.
Breathing, awake or sleeping, he stands there,
the silent one, in the pause at the crest of the breath. Yet how

it longs to curl in on itself at night, that open hand.
Fetched by fate every morning, every day
deferred: by turns abject, immensely fragile, clear.

Til at last an astonished observer begins to understand
and praise it. In words only a poet can say.
And only a god can hear.

---

[32] In poems II, 19 – II, 22, Rilke again seems to be contemplating the distinction between things and people, raising existential questions of meaning, destiny, fate, and meditating on our uneasy relationship with the other phenomena of the world in which we find ourselves.

II, 20

Zwischen den Sternen, wie weit; und doch, um wievieles noch weiter,
was man am Hiesigen lernt.
Einer, zum Beispiel, ein Kind...und ein Nächster, ein Zweiter – ,
o wie unfäßlich entfernt.

Schicksal, es miß uns vielleicht mit des Seienden Spanne,
daß es uns fremd erscheint;
denk, wieviel Spannen allein vom Mädchen zu Manne,
wenn es ihn meidet und meint.

Alles ist weit – , und nirgens schließt sich der Kreis.
Sieh in der Schüssel, auf heiter bereitetem Tische,
seltsam der Fische Gesicht.

Fische sind stumm..., meinte man einmal. Wer weiß?
Aber ist nicht am Ende ein Ort, wo man das, was der Fischen
Sprache wäre, *ohne* sie spricht?

II, 20

Between the stars what measureless infinity.
What greater abysses divide
us from each other. Set one child beside a second, and see
a vastness, unbridgeably wide.

Because we miss fate so, in our beings' brief span,
she now seems a stranger.
Consider, what lengths spring up just between woman and man
if either senses danger.

All is distance; nowhere is the circle closed.
Look, on the gaily spread table, into the dish:
the utterly uncanny visage

of a fish. It's said that they are mute...who knows?
But could one not speak *with* the fish,
without words, there, in its own language?

II, 21

Singe die Gärten, mein Herz, die du nicht kennst; wie in Glas
eingegossene Gärten, klar, unerreichbar.
Wasser und Rosen von Ispahan oder Schiras,
singe sie selig, preise sie, keinem vergleichbar.

Zeige, mein Herz, daß du sie niemals entbehrst.
Daß sie dich meinen, ihre reifenden Feigen.
Daß du mit ihren, zwischen den blühenden Zweigen
wie zum Gesicht gesteigerten Lüften verkehrst.

Meide den Irrtum, daß es Entbehrungen gebe
für den geschehnen Entschluß, diesen: zu sein!
Seidener Faden, kamst du hinein ins Gewebe.

Welchem der Bilder du auch im Innern geeint bist
(sei es selbst ein Moment aus dem Leben der Pein),
fühl, daß der ganze, der rühmliche Teppich gemeint ist.

II, 21

Sing, my heart, of the gardens you do not know;
water poured out into glass, unattainable, clear.
Of the angular patterns of Shiraz, or yet of the roses
of Ispahan sing, praise the beauty without compare.

And show, my heart, how *you* never drew back from them,
how, like a freshening breeze playing over the face,
amongst fruit meant for you, you came and went,
among those ripening figs and budding sprays.

Flee the false thought that somehow you defined
as lack, as loss, your firm resolve: to be!
Silken strand, inwoven from behind.

And in that image which binds up your soul
(be it brief respite from life's agony),
know the glorious tapestry turned, to show the whole.

II, 22

O trotz Schicksal: die herrlichen Überflüsse
unseres Daseins, in Parken übergeschäumt, –
oder als steinerne Männer neben die Schlüsse
hoher Portale, unter Balkone gebäumt!

O die eherne Glocke, die ihre Keule
täglich wider den stumpfen Alltag hebt.
Oder die *eine*, in Karnak, die Säule, die Säule,
die fast ewige Tempel überlebt.

Heute stürzen die Überschüsse, dieselben,
nur noch als Eile vorbei, aus dem waagrechten gelben
Tag in die blendend mit Licht übertriebene Nacht.

Aber das Rasen zergeht und läßt keine Spuren.
Kurven des Flugs durch die Luft und die, die sie führen,
keine vielleicht ist umsonst. Doch nur wie gedacht.

II, 22

What glorious defiance of destiny: our splendidly
extravagant being, flowing over in park
fountains or rearing up fierce, beneath balconies,
before great portals, like grim marble guards.

Or in bells, who raise their bronze mallets to shatter
the torpor of daily routine. Or in Karnak, that one
pillar, the temple's sole survivor, the pillar
that reaches towards eternity, all undone

now by haste – what is left gives way
to speed, the golden horizon of the day.

Haste vanishes too, and leaves no trace.
The curving thrust, what made it soar through space –
none of this is in vain. It is all pure flight.

II, 23

Rufe mich zu jener deiner Stunden,
die dir unaufhörlich widersteht:
flehend nah wie das Gesicht von Hunden,
aber immer wieder weggedreht,

wenn du meinst, sie endlich zu erfassen.
So Entzognes ist am meisten dein.
Wir sind frei. Wir wurden dort entlassen,
wo wir meinten, erst begrüßt zu sein.

Bang verlangen wir nach einem Halte,
wir zu Jungen manchmal für das Alte
und zu alt für das, was niemals war.

Wir, gerecht nur, wo wir dennoch preisen,
weil wir, ach, der Ast sind und das Eisen
und das Süße reifender Gefahr.

II, 23[33]

Summon me, I will come. For all those
hours which so ceaselessly resist
you – like begging dogs, pull in close,
pleading, then pull away again, twist

out of your grasp just when you think you have them.
What is truly yours eludes you. So
we pass through freely, are dismissed just when
we thought we had found welcome. So,

uneasy, we long for safe haven, for rest,
at times too young for what is past,
yet too old for all that is to come.

Who are righteous only if we in praising know
that we ourselves are both the branch and saw
and the sweet danger by which we are undone.

---

[33] In his accompanying notes, Rilke states that II, 23, is addressed to the reader.

II, 24

O diese Lust, immer neu, aus gelockertem Lehm!
Niemand beinah hat den frühesten Wagern geholfen.
Städte entstanden trotzdem an beseligten Golfen,
Wasser und Öl füllten die Krüge trotzdem.

Götter, wir planen sie erst in erkühnten Entwürfen,
die uns das mürrische Schicksal wieder zerstört.
Aber sie sind die Unsterblichen. Sehet, wir dürfen
jenen erhorchen, der uns am Ende erhört.

Wir, ein Geschlecht durch Jahrtausende: Mütter und Väter,
immer erfüllter von dem künftigen Kind,
daß es uns einst, übersteigend, erschüttere, später.

Wir, wir unendlich Gewagten, was haben wir Zeit!
Und nur der schweigsame Tod, der weiß, was wir sind
und was er immer gewinnt, wenn er uns leiht.

II, 24[34]

What delight, ever new, arises from mere clay!
Though no one encouraged the first one who dared,
 still, cities sprang up along Elysian bays,
 still, water and oil between the jugs were shared.

We sketched the gods out first in tentative lines
 destroyed, time and again, by surly fate.
 Ah, but they were immortal. You will find
 they have our ear who hear *us*, soon or late.

Our lineage stretches back for generations,
each mother and father fulfilled in the future's youth,
 who jar us, pushing past. But overtaken,

 we who are ventured, we rule time! And Death
 alone, silent broker, knows our worth,
 and what he gains, when he redeems our pledge.

---

[34] This is the complement to 'Spring Melody' of I, 21.

II, 25

Schon, horch, hörst du der ersten Harken
Arbeit; wieder den menschlichen Takt
in der verhaltenen Still der starken
Vorfrühlingserde. Unabgeschmackt

scheint dir das Kommende. Jenes so oft
dir schon Gekommene scheint dir zu kommen
wieder wie Neues. Immer erhofft,
nahmst du es niemals. Es hat dich genommen.

Selbst die Blätter durchwinterter Eichen
scheinen im Abend ein künftiges Braun.
Manchmal geben sich Lüfte ein Zeichen.

Schwarz sind die Sträucher. Doch Haufen von Dünger
lagern als satteres Schwarz in den Au'n.
Jede Stunde, die hingeht, wird jünger.

II, 25

Listen – you catch the first strike of the plough:
human toil already drumming
hard earth. She holds her breath, waits now
in spring silence. For what is coming

seems untasted. What recurs
again, again, each time seems new.
And while you long for its return,
still you never grasp it. It has seized you.

The winter-clinging oak leaves glint
a foreboding brown in the evening light.
At times the breezes breathe a hint.

The bushes loom black. And dung-heaps fill
the eye a richer midnight. While
each moment falls backward, it grows later still.

II, 26

Wie ergreift uns der Vogelschrei...
Irgend ein einmal erschaffenes Schreien.
Aber die Kinder schon, spielend im Freien,
Schreien an wirklichen Schreien vorbei.

Schreien den Zufall. In Zwischenräume
dieses, des Weltraums (in welchen der heile
Vogelschrei eingeht, wie Menschen in Träume –),
treiben sie ihre, des Kreischens, Keile.

Wehe, wo sind wir? Immer noch freier,
wie die losgerissenen Drachen
jagen wir halbhoch, mit Rändern von Lachen,

windig zerfetzten. – Ordne die Schreier,
singerder Gott! daß sie rauschend erwachen,
tragend als Strömung das Haupt und die Leier.

II, 26

How a bird's scream snares our heart...
Any one of those full cries.
Children, playing in open air,
screech, screech, shriek, run by,

calling out to chance. They seem
to drive deep into this world's hollows
(into which all bird-cries shrink, like people in dreams)
the wedges of their keening. Although

we, alas, are ever more free.
Sheering halfway to heaven like kites ripped loose,
or edges, curling like laughter, all torn to

shreds by the wind. – Gather, o god of melody,
those who cry! That they wake, break loose,
bearing head and lyre before them, on the stream.

II, 27

Gibt es wirklich die Zeit, die zerstörende?
Wann, auf dem ruhenden Berg, zerbricht sie die Burg?
Dieses Herz, das unendlich den Göttern gehörende,
wann vergewaltigts der Demiurg?

Sind wir wirklich so ängstlich Zerbrechliche,
wie das Schicksal uns wahr machen will?
Ist die Kindheit, die tiefe, versprechliche,
in den Wurzeln – später – still?

Ach, das Gespenst des Vergänglichen,
durch den arglos Empfänglichen
geht es, als wär es ein Rauch.

Als die, die wir sind, als die Treibenden,
gelten wir doch bei bleibenden
Kräften als göttlicher Brauch.

II, 27

Does Time, the ravager, really exist?
When will he plunder the tranquil mountain tower?
When will he rape this heart, extinguish
what belongs forever to the god of power?

Fate would have us brittle, anxious,
but are we so, in deepest truth?
Doesn't childhood, deep with promise,
lie fallow in us – still – at root?

Ah, the spectre of long ago –
how it rises like smoke
with youth's guileless thoughts.

As though we who thrust forward could, we too,
among enduring powers, be proved
instruments, for the use of the gods.

II, 28

O komm und geh. Du, fast noch Kind, ergänze
für einen Augenblick die Tanzfigur
zum reinen Sternbild einer jener Tänze,
darin wir die dumpf ordnende Natur

vergänglich übertreffen. Denn sie regte
sich völlig hörend nur, da Orpheus sang.
Du warst noch die von damals her Bewegte
und leicht befremdet, wenn ein Baum sich lang

besann, mit dir nach dem Gehör zu gehn.
Du wußtest noch die Stelle, wo die Leier
sich tönend hob – ; die unerhörte Mitte.

Für sie versuchtest du die schönen Schritte
und hofftest, einmal zu er heilen Feier
des Freundes Gang und Antlitz hinzudrehn.

II, 28

In, out. For one heartbeat, thou almost-child,
  strike up for us and hold that dance's lines
  by which pure constellation, undefiled,
    we fleetingly escape the dull confines

of Nature. That Orpheus would sing
once roused her full awake. And you, thus stirred,
  scarce wondered when a tree, considering,
    paused, then followed you as if it heard

and caught by heart the lute's reverberation
  at that ungranted core where it ascends.
  And so you stretched yourself into the dance,

hoping to draw with you the countenance
  and gait – just once – of that loved friend
    into the healing, saving celebration.

II, 29

Stiller Freund der vielen Fernen, fühle
wie dein Atem noch den Raum vermehrt.
Im Gebälk der finstern Glockenstühle
laß dich läuten. Das, was an dir zehrt,

wird ein Starkes über dieser Nahrung.
Geh in der Verwandlung aus und ein.
Was ist dein leidenste Erfahrung?
Ist dir Trinken bitter, werde Wein.

Sei in dieser Nacht aus Übermaß
Zauberkraft am Kreuzweg deiner Sinne,
ihre seltsamen Begegnung Sinn.

Und wenn dich das Irdische vergaß,
zu der stillen Erde sag: Ich rinne.
Zu dem raschen Wasser sprich: Ich bin.

II, 29[35]

Silent friend of far horizons, feel
how your breath expands the encircling space.
Into the darkened belfry rafters peal
your carillon. Yet what eats away

at you still flourishes. As you drift
in and out of transformation, find:
what knowledge wounds you most? And if
the cup is bitter, change yourself to wine.

Be, in this night of abundance, alchemy –
distilling at the crossroads of your soul
a meaning from this strange encounter – and

then, when all this world forgets you, greet
the silent earth, declaring: still, I flow.
And to the racing water: here I am.

---

[35] As the cycle comes to a close, a hopeful note returns. Even if we are caught in the dilemma of being simultaneously a part of and apart from the earth, perhaps attention to beauty can lift us out of bondage. And perhaps Vera is one example of this transfiguration. The final sonnet, like all good philosophical texts, ends in mystery. Rilke says, enigmatically, that it is addressed to 'a friend of Vera's.' Who is the 'silent friend of far horizons'? Could it be God? The poet? The reader?

About the Translator

Nancy Billias is Professor of Philosophy Emerita from the University of Saint Joseph in Connecticut. Her doctoral dissertation, on Heidegger's philosophy of translation and language, asked: What might poetry, and translation, reveal about our being in the world?

After undertaking careers in social work, psychotherapy, and academia, she has retired to the United Kingdom, where she lives and works as a member of Pilsdon at Malling, an intentional Christian community which offers refuge to people working through depression, alcoholism, addiction, divorce or bereavement.